Books and the City

Books and the City

Psychogeographical Wanderings around Toronto's Independent Bookstores

by

Annabel Townsend

To Shawn Micallef,
I'm sorry for making it weird,
and
to all the indie booksellers of Toronto. Keep up the good fight!

Contents

The Beating Heart of the Literary World

In the shadows of the city, where the neon lights flicker and the streets hum with the whispered secrets of the night, there lies a place of wonder and mystery. It is a place where the shelves are stacked high with stories untold, where the air is thick with the scent of ink and paper, and where the promise of adventure hangs heavy in the air. This place, dear reader, is an independent bookstore.

At least, it is for now.

There are certainly shadowy areas of Regina, Saskatchewan, but we are somewhat lacking in the atmospheric neon lights department particularly in my leafy suburban neighbourhood. If you are picturing a sprawling urban metropolis splashed with unrelenting rain, high rises soaring skywards and a gritty noir drama unfolding in the shadows, then you are sorely mistaken. But we do now have a bookstore. That will always add a little drama.

As a writer, it is my prerogative to engage in a spot of hyperbole. Thus: independent bookstores are the beating heart of the literary world, the keepers of the flame that burns bright in the darkness. They are the guardians of stories, the purveyors of dreams, and the champions of the written word. In these hallowed halls, you can find magic.

An independent bookstore is not just a place to buy books. It is a place to lose yourself in the labyrinth of the imagination, to wander the corridors of the mind, and to discover worlds beyond your wildest dreams. You will discover kindred spirits who share a love of literature, who understand the power of a well-told tale, and who are eager to share their passion with you.

It is also a place that Regina lacked. And so, four years ago, I decided to do something about it.

These sanctuaries of literature have long been cherished by book lovers for their unique charm, personalised service, and curated selections. Often, there is a cat involved as well. My small team at the store have done our best to embody the ideals of a bookstore, but it is a daunting task. Booklovers are highly opinionated folks. Who was I to know what people wanted to read? Where does one begin? The answer came simply: let the customers tell me. Because they always will. Whenever people request a special order from us, we order three copies and add the spares to our shelves. Our stock slowly morphs and evolves into a manifestation of the collective consciousness of our customers that mirrors their every whim. It is a fascinating process to behold.

Owning a bookstore is not, and never has been, easy. Even before the onset of the global pandemic, the independent bookstore industry has faced a myriad of challenges that threaten its very existence in recent years. I speak of course, of The Dread Beast of Bezos. My parents' adolescence was shaped by the Space Race. In turn, I get to watch the man who kills bookstores ride a dildo into orbit.

The combined forces of online retail behemoths, algorithms that predict your interests and desires and the recent need for contactless deliveries, not to mention the costs of running a physical store that still employs humans, provide a terrifying army of foes to be overcome by the humble bookseller. Us 'indies' came together as the industry's underdogs. A ragged band of unlikely heroes battling for what we know to be right and true.

Now, we've reached the point in the lengthy saga where we encounter AI. An unpredictable, soulless enemy that steals from us and then learns from what it has stolen. AI has the potential to render our industry obsolete before we even realise its true power. We are stumbling blindly into the science fiction section, and the robots are already taking over.

But let us not forget the magic of a bookstore, for we have magic on our side. It's in the whispered conversations between books on the shelves, and in how a story can transport you to another world. A simple book can change your life forever. To this end, I have embarked on an epic quest: to seek out my fellow booksellers, to share in their stories, and to proudly join the resistance.

So, dear reader, the next time you pass by an independent bookstore, pause for a moment and step inside. Immerse yourself in the magic that lies within its walls and let yourself be carried away on a sea of words. For in these hidden havens of the written word, you will find not just books, but worlds upon worlds of endless possibilities waiting to be explored.

The Sad Story of CEBA

Once upon a time, I opened a bookstore business, in Regina, Saskatchewan. A week later, the COVID-19 pandemic was declared.

My bookselling dreams came about almost by accident — as all the best adventures do. I had first begun my entrepreneurial career with a coffee shop in 2009, but as a lifelong book lover and aspiring writer, books soon followed me into the cafe in the form of a large book exchange. In the years since then, I'd opened a few other coffee shop ventures. Those cafe ventures did not prove very successful, and I struggled to find ways of making my venture stand out. I realized there are a great many coffee shops in Regina, but very few bookstores. Slowly, an idea formed. Instead of a coffee shop with books in it, I switched to a book shop with a coffee bar in it.

It was the best of times, it was the worst of times…

When the pandemic hit, I didn't shelve my entrepreneurial plans, although they did twist and change considerably as we all learned to cope with those strange times. My book venture grew, not in spite of COVID-19 but perhaps because of it. When else but during lockdown would people get around to reading their 'To Be Read' piles? And what better time to immerse yourself in a fantasy world than when the real world comes to a grinding halt? Suddenly, books were in high demand.

Fast-forward four years, and times are still exceedingly hard in retail. So, in general, people are buying fewer books. However, we are still buying fiction. We all need a good dose of escapism; fiction is wonderful because reality is increasingly unpleasant.

Fiction is not my forte when it comes to writing, but I feel I should turn my adventures with the bookstore business into some sort of comedic farce. Circumstances have been too ridiculous recently for anyone to believe them if I wrote our stories as nonfiction.

It was a dark and stormy night…

Pathetic fallacy is a good literary technique to employ in Saskatchewan winters: this February morning I cycled to work in the snow, feeling appropriately bleak and bitter about the world as befits the frigid environment. It was -28℃ with a -41℃ windchill. My eyelashes frosted over, giving me a cute makeover with Canadian Mascara.

'Entrepreneurship requires dedication,' I tell myself as I pedal, fingers and toes aching with cold. Once safely indoors and thawing, I check our orders. Online orders requiring delivery kept us afloat during the pandemic lockdowns in the first few years of business, but since the restrictions have been lifted, they have tailed off as people returned to in-person shopping. There are only two bookish deliveries to do this week, but unfortunately they are on opposite sides of the city. Roughly a 22 km round trip, or, in this weather, about 90 minutes of cycling. Dedication, dedication… (For the record, I can't drive. The subzero cycling is a matter of necessity rather than choice.)

I try to convince myself that I will acclimatize soon. We have survived four winters in business already. Four insane holiday seasons which, although starting later and later each year, have been enough to keep us going. Four Januarys with 'record-breaking' extremes of temperature. 1,014 km of deliveries clocked on my bicycle computer. Four years of keeping track of public health mandates, masking, capacity restrictions, checking vaccination statuses, interest rate hikes, inflation, adapting, pivoting, leaping through hoops. We have coped with so much already. The worst is supposedly over, and I am absolutely determined not to let this winter be the one that breaks us.

But every story needs a good villain. In mine, the villain arrived in the form of the CEBA (Canadian Emergency Business Account) loan repayment date. The Federal government decided we were all in crisis in 2021 and gave us a lifeline in the form of large loans with a forgivable portion, so long as the bulk was paid off by an arbitrarily set date. That date arrived in mid-January 2024, and we were definitely not prepared for it. We weren't alone, either. Only a tiny fraction of CEBA loan recipients had paid back the money in full. The vast majority, like me, hadn't paid a single penny of it yet. Arguably, we are doing worse in terms of profitability now than we were when we were granted the loans.

Suspend your disbelief, dear reader, as I discovered *I had to raise forty thousand dollars in just eighteen days.*

Together with my family, friends, and staff, we brainstormed madcap, far-fetched schemes to come up with the money quickly. We could forge Hemingway's signature and auction off a fake first edition! I could write smut under a pseudonym and make my fortune with spicy ebooks! I'm sure the thought occurred to some of us, but at no point did we discuss kidnapping Margaret Atwood and holding her for ransom: this is a farce, not a heist novel.

Booksellers are blessed by being surrounded with creative inspiration, and I'm sure our stock holds the answers to all of life's difficulties, if we only know where to look. But the truth of entrepreneurship is stranger than fiction and involves more nerve-wracking drama and conflict than any thriller novel.

Christmas 2023 was one of the most stressful and miserable times of my life, made harder by feeling obliged to hide my stress from my family who were excited to be celebrating the season. I faced losing everything: my job, which was all-encompassing, both business locations, a colossal amount of money, my staff who are all my friends as well, and everything I'd worked so hard to build up over so many years. At my lowest, I was also convinced my husband would leave me because I was so much of a failure. It stung that I was facing this despite overcoming every other hurdle thrown at us during a global pandemic. Hadn't we suffered enough?

Not wishing to end my tall tale on a cliffhanger, I'll conclude that I managed to solve the immediate problem by borrowing huge sums on a line of credit, which makes for a less interesting narrative. But most importantly, it saved the bookstore business, and gives us the opportunity for a sequel. I only hope that other small businesses are as lucky as us when it comes to dealing with the current economic climate, but I know that not everyone will live Happily Ever After.

But for now, my business can turn the page on CEBA, begin a new chapter, and we encourage you all to read on…

Wanderings of the Heart

I had an affair.

I have been so comfortable, happy, and above all, content with my home in Saskatchewan. Regina offers me everything I need – security, loyalty, support, and loving companionship. It's dependable, easy, cozy, and undemanding. We've been together for over a decade, and we just seem to fit.

But at long last, my eye was caught by bigger city lights. Toronto! I craved excitement and adventure, and needed a distraction. The familiar comforts of home were beginning to dull and become suffocating. I was restless.

It was not love at first sight. We caught the briefest glimpses of each other over many years, as I travelled back and forth, always faithfully returning to my first love. Those glimpses did not inspire much attraction: I felt I only ever saw their worst side, and I was always in a hurry. When we were first introduced properly, on a real visit rather than a chance encounter, I had my children with me. They were too hot, too tired, and didn't want to stay long. The city was uninterested in accommodating them, and I had brought too much baggage, literally and figuratively. Our first impressions were not good ones. That time, I was relieved to return home.

But over time, the allure grew. The first time we were alone together was enough; I was infatuated. I wanted more. It all happened so fast. There was so much to explore, each part more fascinating than the next. I wanted to breathe in the scents, drink up the exotic new sensations, and become intoxicated by it all. I knew I wasn't the first, and not the only one to be seduced, but I couldn't help myself. I made excuses, planned, and schemed and arranged a secret rendezvous.

The affair was passionate but ultimately futile. That which burns brightest, fades quickest. My brief dalliance left me reeling and exhausted, disheveled but satiated. I knew then that this was an act of hedonism; casual, temporary, and frivolous. Not a relationship that could be sustained.

Curiosity abated, I was glad to at last return home feeling more than a little sheepish. To my relief, I was forgiven and welcomed back to my safe and sleepy prairie.

Toronto, I love you, but I can't live with you.

* * *

Despite solving my immediate financial crisis with the bookstore business, the weather, the financial woes, and the stress-induced insomnia all took their toll on me. As New Year dawned in 2024, I was in desperate need of a break. Unfortunately, breaks are very difficult things to engineer when you are a full time 'solopreneur' or whatever the buzzword currently is for someone who works themselves into a stupor. A holiday was the last thing I could afford at that moment. Instead, I found a corporate trade show in Mississauga held at the end of January. The Trade Show did include book and stationary companies, and so with a bit of creative licence, I could justify it as a legitimate business expense. And of course, I wouldn't actually stay in Mississauga… no one stays in Mississauga if they have a choice.

I got my tickets as an official Purchaser for the bookstore and flew to Toronto Pearson airport on the red-eye flight from Regina. Business-like I was not: it has been nearly two decades since I could plausibly consider myself an authentic student backpacker, but yet the scruffy, overstuffed backpack with the obligatory maple leaf patch came with me around this highly corporate exhibition. I told myself I needed it for gathering samples of new stock I would inevitably end up purchasing for the store. I noticed that everyone else brought smart little wheeled suitcases that could be towed one handed while brandishing a huge travel mug in the other.

The trade show was a short ride from the airport, and I think I was the only registered guest to arrive by bus. Throughout the ten-minute journey, I did not spot a single feature on the landscape that was not grey. A seemingly endless highway filled with white and silver SUVs, utilitarian warehouses and soulless airport hotels with windows staring like the compound eyes of a giant dusty moth. The clouded sky mirrored the colour of the ubiquitous concrete, and the little snow that persisted was stained with the collective pollutants from the airport and the road. Grubby pigeons clustered on the overpass. The only colour came from giant, flickering billboards suspended over the cars, and the cheery red Tim Hortons cups that littered the sidewalks. If armpits were grey, Mississauga would be an armpit.

The show was about as useful as I expected it to be; the majority in attendance were well-intentioned, well-heeled, and well-off women from major fashion retailers: the type who recognise, and care about, the differences between specific brands of leather handbag. I bought notebooks and appreciated the free champagne, but I was done with stumbling aimlessly around the colossal hall of minimalist gold jewellery and monochrome abstract art prints in one afternoon.

That gave me two more blissful days of wandering around downtown Toronto, seeking out as many indie bookstores as I was able. I wanted to see the big city, and I badly needed a change of scenery from the grim prairie winter. I sought solace in solo wanderings, too. I wanted to find inspiration to improve my situation at home, comradery in others experiencing the same difficulties, and to see how fellow booksellers were coping through these cruel and unusual times.

Above all, I was looking for Hope.

Psychogeography

Handwritten cue cards litter the floor, dropped and scattered in a fit of frustration. "It's all crap! I hate this!" he complains. "I've got like, one paragraph and the rest is just boring!"

In my current role in life, these sentiments are not unusual to hear. The self-doubt of writers is almost universal. What is unusual is that these shouts are coming from my thirteen-year-old, the cue cards are written entirely in French, and the topic in which he has got stuck is *psychogeography*.

I am immensely proud, despite the mess on the floor. There can't be many young teenagers who are willing to do a presentation about psychogeography in their second language, in front of a large class of their rowdy Grade 8 peers. I think he even surprised the teacher with this one.

I cannot read French, and so Milo's conclusions about psychogeography remain a mystery to me, but we did have some interesting discussions. I am unaware what prompted his interest, but I can take some strategic guesses. My husband works as a cartographer, using hard data, complex mathematics, and computer modelling to create maps of real physical spaces. In sharp contrast, I spend my time stomping around viewing our neighbourhood and community through a semi-conscious lens of anthropology, and then filtering my experiences into world-building in my writing. Milo has said he wants to be a psychologist when he grows up. Consequently, the psychogeography school project seems a natural amalgamation of our family's interests.

The discipline of psychogeography is a concept as enigmatic as the cities it seeks to unravel. Milo and I had difficulties deciding on a working definition. Coined by the avant-garde movement known as 'Situationist International' in the 1950s, psychogeography defies conventional cartography, (much to my husband's consternation), instead embracing the subjective experience of urban spaces.

At its core, and much like our family, psychogeography is a marriage of psychology and geography but with a good dose of creativity and ethnography thrown in. It is a practice that seeks to explore the effect of geographical surroundings on the emotions and behaviour of the people living in it. It is a lens through which we can view a place not as a static, lifeless entity, but as a living, breathing organism that shapes and is shaped by the people who inhabit it.

For once, Milo's French classes come in useful. To understand psychogeography, one must first embrace the concept of the *dérive,* a French term which roughly translates to "drift" or "drifting." The *dérive* is more than just a leisurely stroll through the city; it is a deliberate act of unplanned wandering, a surrender to the whims of the urban landscape. Or, often as not, simply "to get lost deliberately," as I explained to Milo. During a *dérive,* a psychogeographer is encouraged to let go of preconceived notions of space and time, to follow the path that calls out to them, whether it be a bustling street or a quiet alleyway. In doing so, they can uncover hidden narratives and forgotten histories, revealing the city in all its glory.

"So, it's basically just exploring for introverts?" asks Milo.

He is not wrong.

Through the *dérive*, psychogeography invites us to reimagine our relationship with the city, to see it not as a mere backdrop to our lives, but as a canvas upon which our stories are written. In my bookish world, there are countless examples in literature where the city becomes a character in its own right. Think of Pratchett's Ankh Morpork in the *Discworld*, the fictionalised version of Oslo in Jo Nesbo's *Harry Hole* series, and even Rebus's Edinburgh (Ian Rankin). Perhaps unbeknownst to them, the authors are all writing psychogeography, albeit of fictional cities. The discipline challenges us to question the boundaries and divisions that define urban spaces, encouraging us to forge our own paths and create our own narratives.

Ultimately, psychogeography is a reminder that the city or neighbourhood is more than just a collection of buildings and streets; it is a reflection of our collective consciousness, a mirror that reveals our hopes, fears, and dreams. It is a call to adventure, an invitation to explore the unknown, and a reminder that even in the most familiar of places, there is always something new to discover.

The Search for Shawn Micallef

Having already begun an illicit affair with Toronto and managed to emotionally reconcile it with my loyalty to Saskatchewan, I thought I could continue the secretive liaisons without remorse. To this end, I am now stalking a man who knows a few things about wandering around the city.

He has no idea who I am, we've never spoken, but I've seen him. I know he likes wearing bowties. I've seen photos of his sweet family, his holidays, even his bicycle. I know where he works, and most significantly, I know exactly which routes he takes to get to work.

I know all this because he wrote it down for me. He even included maps and gave directions for his fans to follow him.

His name is Shawn.

In 2022, I attended the Toronto International Festival of Authors (TIFA) for the first time. An idea was already forming in my head about psychogeography writings, and so I attended the TIFA 'Critical Conversations' event on the topic of 'Affordable Cities.' Toronto is not a prime example of affordable living, obviously, and I was curious to see if any of these big city folks would even mention the likes of Regina in comparison. The event was a panel discussion, covering topics like affordable housing (or lack of it), the recent mayoral race, and who uses the transit system versus who designs it. I settled into the plush red chair at the Studio at the Harbourfront auditorium, my name badge and access pass getting tangled in my hair in the darkness. The lights came up on the stage and my heart skipped a beat… *there he was!*

Shawn Micallef is the author of *Frontier City: Toronto on the Verge of Greatness,* a book from 2016 that I quickly bought at the TIFA book fair. He's also a psychogeographer who writes columns for the Toronto Star and founded *Spacing* magazine. But most significantly, he wrote a book called *Stroll* in 2010. *Stroll* is about wandering aimlessly around Toronto with hand-drawn maps. It is about people and habits and the environment and politics (and Politics) and movement and space and design and community and architecture and cycling and wayfinding and transit and storytelling and history and lived experience. In short, all the things that absolutely fascinate me.

> *"Shawn Micallef looks at the city in a way we all should more often – he sees it as a living book that is alive with stories just waiting to be told to the attentive observer."* – David Crombie, former mayor of Toronto.

I decided at that instant that I wanted, nay, *needed* that book. Immediately after the talk, I ran to the TIFA bookstore. Unfortunately, the cashier was not aware that this book was part of the festival and they hadn't stocked it. I could try the big Indigo in the Eaton Centre? she suggested. I did consider it, but then decided I had not come all this way just to go to Indigo. I owned a bookstore. I could just order it in from Regina and pay wholesale rates.[1]

Over the next few days, I had increasingly outlandish literary adventures at TIFA. I ventured out on a Happiness Collection Walk with a girl wearing a red foam rubber nose, joined the audience for a live recording of CBC's *Writers and*

---

[1] Disclaimer:

It is 2024 and, for better or worse, I am on the internet almost constantly. I still follow Shawn on Instagram. I am aware that I could just slide into his DMs. Or buy *Stroll* off Thrift Books, maybe.

But that is not how the best adventures begin.

Company, and talked to a group of children about Axolotls with a Swedish woman who had flown in just for the occasion. I also got utterly, hopelessly lost in the rain on more than one occasion. By the time I returned to Regina, I confess, I had completely forgotten about ordering *Stroll.*

However, I began amiably stalking Shawn Micallef on Instagram. A year passed, and then he posted… *Stroll!* But with a new cover. Coming in 2024, an updated version of *Stroll* is to be published. Whereas I will no doubt buy the new release when the time comes, this means that the older first edition is now being pulled from the publisher's listings, and it is getting harder and harder to buy. This reminder became a catalyst: I was now more determined than ever to find and acquire the original 2010 *Stroll.* What's more, I thought, I would go back to Toronto to find it. And maybe even track down Shawn himself. He literally gave me a map, after all….

Part 1: South

Bad Beginnings: Potatoes, Penguins, and Coffee

It was 2019, the summer before the world turned upside down. My family and I had been in Canada for seven years and had never yet spent any time in the country's first city. It was time to change that, we thought. Especially since my parents were visiting from the UK and had to fly into Toronto anyway. We met them at Pearson airport, and rented out an expensive AirBnB condo that slept all six of us, uncomfortably. It was right in the downtown core, 'in spitting distance' of the CN Tower, as my mother put it. (I did not, in fact, spit at the Tower). It was July, humid; the temperature never dipped below 30 degrees all week. The heat turned family dynamics increasingly fraught. We found the whole city stifling, noisy, prohibitively expensive, and largely inaccessible when navigating with a tired, hot four-year-old and a senior with bad knees in tow.

On that trip, I was partially 'celebrating' my new-found freedom. The week before, I had quit my job. I had been working at the Saskatchewan Science Centre for the previous two years, as the Community Programs Coordinator. I genuinely loved it: where else would you get the opportunity to be paid for persuading people to launch potatoes into Wascana Lake using homemade rocket launchers?[2] Or make 25 life-sized and anatomically correct

---

[2] Coincidentally, a friend of mine works at the University of Regina as a paleoliminologist. That is, he studies fossilized lake beds, which is exactly what the city of Regina is sitting on – which in turn explains its total lack of topography. As part of his research, my friend regularly has to do chemical analysis of Wascana Lake water. The anomalous, increased Potassium levels found after my potato rockets escapade have been forever immortalised as 'The

human brains out of agar jelly, for dissection? Unfortunately, like all third-sector positions, my role was terribly paid and with no prospects of career advancement whatsoever. By 2019, I knew the end was nigh: I was running out of ideas and patience. I wanted to quit before I lost any love for the place. I said fond goodbyes to my equally eccentric colleagues and the Office Crickets (that would later become lunch to Stephen the King Snake), and cycled home around the potato-filled lake for the last time. I was sad to leave, but I felt a brief vacation in Toronto would set me right.

Besides, I had the beginnings of an idea.

My idea was to open my own bookstore. Quite a leap from community science programming admittedly, but never having been one for linear career progression, it did not seem beyond the realms of possibility. By sheer coincidence, I discovered that our Toronto AirBnb was a few blocks from Penguin Random House's headquarters. The major publisher had a little orange-painted and penguin-adorned store front below its enormous office, so I decided to pay them a visit.

When I explained that I wanted to open a bookstore, the Penguin workers immediately started treating me like royalty in their little shop. I bought myself a coffee mug with the original Penguin Paperback Classics cover of *Wuthering Heights* on it, but also came away with a Penguin tote bag full of catalogues of their Fall releases, Penguin stickers and pins, and even some Advance Reader Copies. My family saw me return with my hoard and quietly despaired. At the time, I felt a little bad for talking my way into so many freebies given my bookstore was nothing more than a sketch in my journal. I hadn't even fully explained the concept to my husband then. Nearly five years later, I regret nothing. I

Annabel Factor' (2018) in his peer-reviewed academic journal articles. This was, beyond a doubt, my defining contribution to Science.

think I have spent more than $30,000 at Penguin Random House since that first visit. They definitely owe me a few stickers.

***

2024, and I am back in Toronto, beginning my epic search for Shawn Micallef's *Stroll* book. Since I had little idea of where I was going, using only the CN Tower and Lake Ontario as points of reference to orientate myself, I thought it best to start at the Harbourfront and head up from there. At this point, my voyage wasn't entirely aimless: I had contacted my Penguin Random House sales representative and told her I'd be in the city for a few days, and could I come visit the Penguin HQ? I knew Penguin did not publish *Stroll*, but I decided I couldn't come on a bookstore odyssey and not visit Penguin. My rep seemed surprised by the request, but as she learned that I was, genuinely, a 'purchaser' for a real store, she agreed to meet and promised me a run-down of the publisher's latest offerings for the year. She also told me that, partially as a result of the pandemic, and partly through corporate leases expiring, Penguin no longer ran the little store front under their offices that I had visited before. I was crestfallen – that place was cute and sort of 'what started it all.'

The morning of my intended visit, I woke up bleary eyed and dishevelled, having not gotten much sleep in my cheap hostel room. My first thought was for Coffee, and coffee alone. It was a medical necessity. I shared an Uber ride back towards the southern edge of the city and aimed for Fahrenheit Coffee, which I'd thought was at least somewhere in the general vicinity of Penguin Random House. It was not an easy place to find even despite our Uber driver's expert knowledge. He insisted I was in the right place and shooed me out of the car onto the bottom of Spadina Avenue. I crossed the street, immediately reaching for my phone for Google maps. Unfortunately, Google maps lacked detail – namely the detail that Fahrenheit Coffee is in the basement of a mall with no signage on the outside. Confused, I walked three sides around the mall, past the dumpsters and through the parking lot – a singularly unattractive side of the old red brick building. Spadina Avenue is a major thoroughfare and Fahrenheit Coffee is definitely the hang-out of wealthier urbanites, yet the sketchy-looking alleys and places I would not like to be in at night are just a few feet away. It does not take much to get exceedingly lost in Toronto.

I am not sure if it was because I was so tired, or just because of the general atmosphere and excitement of my trip, but my $7 'Diablo Blend' americano from Fahrenheit was some of the best coffee I've had in years. And of course I met someone to chat with. In the best coffee shops, you always do.

My mental 'Barista Bingo' card filled quickly, (early 20s, floppy hair that he elegantly flicked out of his dewy eyes, eyebrow piercing, forearm tattoos…) and then I heard him speak. A British accent! A very familiar British accent, too. Bingo! A gap-year kid on a working holiday visa, I'm sure. Our eyes met in awkward ex-pat familiarity.

"Whereabouts are you from?" he asked.

I knew he didn't mean Saskatchewan. "Kent," I admitted.

"Yeah, but where in Kent?"

"Ashford."

"You're kidding – I'm from Tonbridge Wells," he grinned.

The British are not a close-knit diaspora by any means, but I'd argue there is nowhere else in the world where you can pinpoint the origin of an accent from a tiny part of a tiny island with such accuracy. Yes, I had crossed the Atlantic, built a life for myself four thousand miles from 'home,' and yet, and yet… I try to go for coffee in a city of six million people, and run into a guy born just 20 miles from where I grew up.

Inevitably, the conversation turned to what on earth I was doing in Toronto, caffeine deprived, off the tourist trail and clutching a large but as-yet empty book bag. Suddenly I realised I was late for meeting my Penguin representative, and rapidly took my leave.

Walking quickly now that I was caffeinated, I headed east along Front Street. With the little bookstore gone, I was less than impressed with Penguin's HQ. It is extremely corporate and intimidating from the outside, and not the sort of place you could wander into hopefully as a wannabe bookseller – a sharp contrast with the cheery orange kiosk from a few years before. I wanted to be awed! This was one of the Big Five publishers, after all. Very few people outside the company ever get to see what goes on inside a publishers' office, and I thought of all the poor hopeless writers who would do anything to get inside these grey featureless corporate walls to sweet-talk the acquisitions editors. I tried to seem impressed, but all I really wanted to do was drink more Fahrenheit Coffee, or maybe just go back to bed. I dutifully collected catalogues again, and feigned interest in the manufactured hype around the forthcoming Sophie Gregoire Trudeau memoir, promising to pre-order for the store in good time. I then made a swift exit.

A disappointing start to my bookstore odyssey, but the next on my list was only a few blocks away.

Books bought: 0
Copies of *Stroll* found: 0
Coffees consumed: 2

David Mason, and why I love TTC

Yet again, I got lost.

David Mason Books, according to my frantic Google searches, is located a couple of blocks north of Front Street and the Penguin Random House office, on Adelaide Street. David Mason Books was founded in the sixties and specialises in antiquarian, rare, and special interest books. I was not going to find a copy of *Stroll* in there!

There is a similar antiquarian book dealer in Regina, and from what I've learned from the owner of that one, most of the antique book business takes place online. This means that antiquarian bookstores tend to be an afterthought. Their clientèle are serious collectors and are generally less concerned with things like logically laid out bookshelves or beautifully curated window displays or racks of new releases. In fact, every one of these stores I've seen so far resembles an eccentric aristocrat's home library. Leather armchairs, old oak furniture, curios filling the gaps between the books. Dust. Threadbare rugs. These are cliches of course, but cliches do originate in reality. David Mason Books at least posts regular opening hours, but this is not always the standard.

The antiquarian store in Regina has a store pet – Oxford the dog. He is locally famous, considerably more well-known than his human owner. This appears to be another trend unique to bookstores: in-store animals. David Mason Books boasts at least two bookstore cats. Most of the online reviews of the place mention the cats, but not the actual books. I was looking forward to meeting them.

David Mason still owns the shop and has even written his own books about the antiquarian book trade. The store, in the exceedingly expensive financial district close to the centre of Toronto, would seem to be doing excellent business. It was one of the first places that showed up when I researched bookstores in Toronto and its reputation precedes it.

But could I find it? No, I could not.

I was definitely on the right street. I followed the little blue dot on Google maps, and even flicked to the Street View so I could see what the outside of the building looked like. It did not help.

David Mason Books appears to be inside an office building, along with several other businesses, some of which were definitely not open to the public. There was no signage on the outside to tell people of the bookstore's existence, or indeed, anything about what lay within. My view from the street was just of stairs, a few shallow ones leading up to a blank hallway with nondescript office doors leading off it, and a longer staircase that curled around a corner and then down below street level. I could not see the names of any of the businesses inside. I stood outside the glass doors, awkwardly fidgeting and wondering for the fifteenth time whether I was on the right side of the street. Finally, a man in a grey suit came out through the doors, and I took my chance.

"Excuse me, is there a bookstore here?"

He seemed surprised, and a little irritated.

"Yes, I think so. With the cat. On the lower floor." And then he was gone.

Hesitantly, I went in and headed down the stairs.

I still could not find David Mason Books. Instead, there was closed blue door after closed blue door. None were labelled. Someone else, also in dress pants and holding files emerged from a door and glared at me. I lost my nerve. I couldn't be in the right place, could I?

I should have stayed and explored. It must have been close. But suddenly the tiredness and caffeine caught up with me and I gave up and stomped back up the stairs in irritation. No cats and old books for me this time.

Maybe I am just too inept, or maybe I was entirely in the wrong place. I will never know, and part of me regrets giving up so easily. But I cannot be alone in getting confused with that place. The bookstore did nothing to make itself obvious. Perhaps it was deliberate? All part of the allure, the secretive hidden shelves, discoverable only to the worthy few. Mr. Mason is either extremely confident in his business model as is, or the bookstore is actively hiding from non-specialists, like me.

Thwarted, I decided to hit "reset" on my bookstore odyssey. Back to the Harbourfront to start over, I thought.

***

I caught a tram. I mean, a streetcar.

As I age, I am becoming more and more comfortable with the realisation that I am a transit enthusiast. In the UK, I hated public transport vehemently, as did everyone else who was forced to rely on the unreliable and afford the unaffordable. UK public transport is so woefully inadequate compared to the systems of our European neighbours that it is a national embarrassment.

However, there were some advantages: I met my husband on a long-distance bus because both of us were too poor to buy train tickets. The shared trauma of ten hours crammed into the putrid confines of the National Express bus from North Wales to Kent was enough to bond us for life. The concept of driving that distance (230 miles, or "just down the road" by Canadian standards), let alone owning a car in which to do so, was simply alien to us then.

I have still never owned a car. I've never even passed my driving test, despite attempts on both sides of the Atlantic. While at university, I once begged a ride from a friendly psychology student. He chose to tell me that I had obviously taken an 'inner vow' against driving and that I would never be able to do it unless I underwent cognitive behavioural therapy to remove this mental block. And then he dropped me at the train station, so I decided to ignore him.

Not driving is a much bigger deal in Canada than in the UK. Most of my friends who've remained in Britain – all of us in our forties now – still do not have cars. It is much less exceptional over there, because as annoying and expensive as the train network is, at least it exists.

I saw an advert for a writers' retreat in rural Saskatchewan recently. The ad confidently advised that the nearest airports to the retreat location were Regina or Calgary. Then it stated: 'There is no public transport in Saskatchewan outside of the urban centres.' I feel that is acutely shameful, which is why, when presented not only with transit courtesy of the renowned TTC, but a choice of forms of transit with Toronto's buses, streetcars, metro trains, and even a bike share option, I was positively giddy.

During my first trip, I downloaded an app that allowed me to unlock Toronto's little green bikes. It took me an afternoon to figure it out, but provided I remembered to change bikes every half an hour, I could cycle everywhere I needed over a three-day period, for $15. Fantastic! My cheap lodgings that time were on Dundas Street West, not far from the Kensington Market area, and there were two bike share points in sight of my room. Once I had got over The Fear of cycling through downtown traffic, I started to really appreciate inner city cycling. Crossing streetcar tracks while helmetless and knowing that a sizeable portion of downtown residents probably hated my green-wheeled existence did little to improve my confidence, but I soon got used to it. Toronto has miles of semi-protected bike lanes. Unlike Regina's pathetic bike 'network,' these bike lines actually took me where I wanted to go. Kensington Market was very cycle-friendly, and I found I could get to the book festival at the Harbourfront from there on a bike in just seven minutes, which I'm fairly sure would have been quicker than driving.

The bikes are heavy things however, designed to be easily identifiable as part of the bike share scheme, and indestructible rather than speedy – presumably making them less tempting to steal as well. They only have three gears. I barely have to use gears at all in Saskatchewan, but I soon discovered that cycling back to the second hostel on Danforth involved a long, slow hill up Jones Avenue. So out of breath was I that it very nearly put me off any more bicycle adventures, and I really could have done with another ring between my pedals.

By the time I arrived back in Toronto for the third time in January, all the bikes had turned orange – the result of a recent rebranding exercise. The appeal of cycling had dulled for me, too. I did not know how those bikes would fare on top of ice. Plus, I thought I would be able to see more on foot. Few of the bookstores on my list had bike racks outside them, anyway. So I walked, but I also bought a Presto card and when I got too frustrated or tired or lost, I got on the bus. I rarely had to look for them or worry about missing them. Stand near a marked stop long enough, and something will show up. I don't think I ever waited longer than five minutes. Such a blissful contrast to Regina, where there is only one bus every half hour, and if you miss it, it can actually be fatal: you risk getting stuck waiting in -20℃. A particularly tragic, grim news story from January this year told of a man who got off the last bus of the night in a Regina suburb, but had a bad fall in the snow and was unable to stand again. He froze to death, just a few feet from the bus stop. Anywhere else, I'm sure some other vehicle would have passed and been able to help him; not so in this sleepy, empty city.

This time, back in Toronto, the sleek silent streetcar transported me effortlessly back down to the Harbourfront, circumventing Union station, which I was very relieved about. (Union Station remains an impenetrable labyrinth for me and I will avoid going anywhere near it if at all possible.) I acquired more coffee, regrouped, and headed off to the next bookstore.

Books bought: 0
Copies of *Stroll* found: 0
Coffees consumed: 2

Nautical Mind

Nautical Mind Bookstore also took some finding, but after my failures with David Mason, I was now determined. I thought I knew the area – Toronto's Harbourfront – fairly well by now having spent two International Festival of Authors weeks there. Even in January, the sunset over the lake is gorgeous, and the evening cityscape dominated by the CN Tower still brings a little thrill of the exotic to me. During the day, the area along Queen's Quay East is spacious, pedestrian-friendly, and attractive. The ever-present smell of deep fried sweet 'Beaver Tails' from the kiosk in the middle coupled with the screeches of gulls immediately puts me in vacation-mode. There is public art all around the Harbourfront Studio Theatre and a full art gallery overlooking the lake. I haven't found any exceptional coffee at the Harbourfront yet, but there is a bar with at least four types of beer named after bicycles, which keeps me happy. Better still, at the ferry terminal that runs boats out to the islands, there is a phenomenal South Asian curry house. Hands down, the best meal I had in the city: rich goat curry and roti and all in a polystyrene container stained neon yellow from the tumeric, for $12.

Just in front of the imposing Queen's Quay terminal building, there is also Toronto Book Garden. Established in 2014, this is a little patch of greenery with brick paths weaving between the plants, interspersed with the names of previous Toronto Book Award winners and the year of their win. These authors are all honoured for their use of 'Toronto' as a concept in their writings, regardless of genre. I recognised many names, but many more were new to me. The stone markers stretch back to 1974, and apparently new ones are added every year. I only hope that award winning authors writing about Toronto aren't too numerous, because the plants and trees there are far prettier than the brick paving.

Nautical Mind proved to be another bookstore unenthusiastic about self-promotion, much like David Mason Books. This time, Google maps was easier to follow, as this bookstore is located close to some major landmarks – namely, the huge Radisson Hotel, a Tim Hortons branch and… the police station. An obvious place for a specialist bookstore.

I had been told in no uncertain terms that I had to find this place, take photographs of it, and, if possible, buy a book there and mail it to the UK. My friend is a keen amateur sailor. Having moved to the west coast of the UK several years ago, she turned a passing interest in tall ships into a passion and has spent most of the past decade salty and wet, tying knots and racing boats around the more exciting parts of Europe. Hearing about her adventures makes me admire her considerably, but I can't say that it sounds like fun, by any stretch of the imagination. If it's sailing books she wants though, it is sailing books she will get.

Snuggled in between the police station and the hotel is an unassuming little place with gridded windows and an ageing wooden sign hanging over the sidewalk engraved with a ship and an anchor. To me, it exuded traditional tattoo vibes rather than books. The windows were crammed full of books however, and most had more boats on the covers.

Inside, I was the only customer. This was not surprising. Two women were waiting patiently behind the counter, and the younger one asked if she could help me find anything. I have no understanding of, and barely any interest in, anything nautical, so I wasn't really sure how to answer. Instead, I introduced myself as a fellow bookstore owner, and said I was glad to find them. I explained my mission to see as many bookstores in Toronto as I could, and then told them about my sea-loving friend.

The older woman turned out to be the owner. Her husband had founded Nautical Mind over thirty years ago, and now she had taken it over. The words echoed around my head. Thirty years! Any small business surviving that long is remarkable enough, but for such a niche business, in such an out-of-sight location, it was incredibly inspiring. When I expressed those thoughts, the owner smiled and confessed that over those decades, the past three years had been the hardest of all. *She* thought *I* was remarkable for having just started in the industry during this difficult period.

She also told me that they class themselves as "Marine Booksellers and Chart Agents" and that most of their trade is in the logs, charts, and maps and intricate manuals full of tidal tracking and the incomprehensible array of data needed at sea. In the age of the internet and satellite phones and all manner of advanced navigation technology, I had no idea that these things were still written down on paper. Somehow, it seemed rather much for the few tourist boats on Lake Ontario, but they were likely the only such store in the province, if not in Canada. Much like David Mason Books, theirs is a small customer base, but they have very few competitors.

Besides those technical publications though, the small store also had a children's section, which surprised me, but then there are children's books on everything if you know where to look. Then I found a singular shelf of adult fiction novels. (No copies of *Moby Dick* or *Twenty-Thousand Leagues Under the Sea*, which admittedly were the only 'sea' books that I could think of in the spur of the moment!). Right under the window, there was even a bargain section.

With the younger woman's sage advice, I picked up a book of *Everyday tips for Skippers* for my friend and was gifted many store-branded bookmarks, too. The women wished me sincere good luck with my business and I returned the sentiments. Nautical Mind Bookstore gave me so much hope. That a place like that could survive, let alone thrive, for thirty years, was awe-inspiring. And if they could do it, so could I.

Feeling invigorated, I wandered out of the store towards the streetcar stop, humming cheerfully to myself. It was only on the crowded streetcar that I realised I was humming *The Last Pirate of Saskatchewan*.

Books bought: 1
Copies of *Stroll* found: 0
Coffees consumed: 1

The City is Art

Somewhere in the 'Entertainment district' of Toronto – that is, near the CN Tower, the Blue Jays stadium, and Nathan Phillips Square (that has the lit-up giant TORONTO sign outside of it and a large skating rink in winter) – lies Grange Park. Engraved into the paving slabs around the edge of the grass are quotes from writers about cities. The first I found was from Jane Jacobs, the author of *The Death and Life of Great American Cities.*

"We and our cities, just by virtue of being, are a legitimate part of nature."

The concrete and brutalist architecture in Toronto may not be the first images that come to mind when you think of 'nature,' but in the present day, cities *are* our natural environment. Most humans – 56% of the world population now – live in urban environments, and that percentage is predicted to rise to 68% by 2050. We are part of nature and, naturally, we have shaped our physical geography into cities.

The word 'psycho-geo-graphy' is constructed from Greek etymology. '-graphy' is 'writing,' '-geo' is 'the world' and 'psych' originally meant 'soul' or 'self' in the sense of 'conscious personality.' So, psycho-geo-graphy is writing about yourself in the world. Or the world as you experience it. The idea of 'writing the world' appeals to me far more than geography classes in high school ever did. Perhaps if they'd explained it in those terms, I would have paid more attention.[3]

Psychogeography is a science and an art. The science is the study and recording of the physical attributes of a place. The art is in the creative writing, but arguably, it is also in the conscious design of our cities in the first place. I am woefully unqualified to write about Toronto's architecture, or even the design of the buildings that house all the bookstores I visited, but I can still appreciate the odd spots of public art that I encountered on route, the effects they had on me, and the emotions and behaviour they evoked.

Toronto has a great deal of public art, randomly tucked into corners or popping up in unexpected places. In the north end, there is an eight-foot-high blue dinosaur, made out of sheet metal and made to look like it had been folded into an origami sculpture. At the time, I was looking for the Toronto Reference Library, which in itself is a work of art. (My sketches of the place do not do it justice!) The five-storey building holds close to four million publications. I am sure that at least one of them explains the proximity of the blue dinosaur.

The reference library is a truly beautiful building to be in, especially surrounded by books and in awed silence. As you enter, a series of staircases unfurls like the tiers of an ancient amphitheatre, leading up to rows of reading desks perched on higher levels, each one an oasis of concentration. A glass elevator transports you up and into the unknown. The library feels alive, a silent, pulsing organism where the rustling of pages blends seamlessly into the air.

---

[3] For the record, I now have a PhD in Geography. I still don't really know how that happened.

The lower floors are an expansive sea of bookshelves, laden with knowledge, yet oddly disorienting as the shelves bend into tight corners and obscure alcoves. It was easy to lose myself among these towering rows—one minute I was skirting around the edge of a bookshelf, and the next, I found myself in a quiet corner full of potted plants, where the outside world felt a thousand miles away. The standard library near-silence carried a strange intimacy, as if each polite footstep of my fellow visitors was an acknowledgment of the shared, sacred space. I sat at a desk on the fourth floor looking out over the atrium for a while, reading something about witches, until the quiet became unnerving and I descended and switched to the attached and much noisier coffee shop. I got my coffee to go, and wandered off again, completely disorientated. Apparently, it is much easier to spot blue dinosaurs when you have no specific destination in mind.

A rival to the blue dinosaur may be the huge bronze 'couch monster' standing on a ball that looms outside the Art Gallery of Ontario. It was designed by Brian Jungen. The 'monster' is a four-metre-tall elephant, but the bronze is worked in a way that looks like the whole thing is constructed from old leather couches. Unfortunately, I found it on a particularly wet and miserable day, and so I automatically preferred the bright blue dinosaur sculpture over the dark and dripping elephant.

Wandering vaguely southwest of the Art Gallery of Ontario eventually leads to the edge of Kensington Market. This area has all sorts of colourful art installations, but even before you enter the neighbourhood, you can pass through what I consider to be physically 'writing the city' – that is, Graffiti Alley. Graffiti Alley, technically 'Rush Lane' on the map, is an alley leading west from Spadina Avenue, running parallel to and just below Queen Street West. I recognised it as being the backdrop of the Rant segments on the *Rick Mercer Report* show, where Mercer paces up and down complaining about things with the camera always tilted at odd angles.

Graffiti Alley is extremely colourful, a chaotic mix of styles and subjects. Seemingly every brick in the kilometre long stretch is covered with some sort of artwork, from the usual tags and scrawled slogans to political cartoons, portraiture and psychedelic abstract patterns. I was particularly fond of a giant raccoon mural wearing a top hat, and an elegant hammerhead shark. The alley ends at the Alex Wilson Community Garden, a little walled green space with a wooden walkway crossing it. The gate at the entrance is decorated with an oversized wooden pencil. Around a corner from the shark someone had written "Get Off The Internet" and I felt like I had found my Happy Place in the city.

Graffiti Alley is quite literally writing *on* the city, rather than just 'writing the city' geographically. The best part about the alley is that it is different for every visitor. There will be something new painted on a previously unadorned patch of brick, or some of the older designs will have been sprayed over or altered on each visit. This city art is ever-changing.

As Shawn Micallef found in having to revise his *Stroll* book, cities are not static. Our cities are still organic and dynamic, growing and changing, both by accident and design. In this sense, psychogeographical accounts of somewhere as *alive* as Toronto are difficult to write, especially given the glacial speed of the publishing industry.[4] By the time this book is finished, many of the things I mention may well have changed; businesses will have closed or moved, new ones will have opened. Things get built and demolished, infrastructure is updated, and the city authorities argue about transit links. Mapping a city is a never-ending task.

I am not a cartographer, but I did marry one. That particular cartographer has tried to show me how maps can be art too. Twenty years ago, I watched my now-husband painstakingly digitise 5,000 square kilometres of South African impact crater site for his undergraduate dissertation, before the days of remote sensing software and Google Earth. The maps and models he produced then were beautiful in an absurdist way, all false-coloured and contoured. I think I admired them more because I had no idea what I was looking at.

The same is true when I encounter modern maps. Both of the Toronto hostels I stayed in had little maps available, free for hapless tourists. To me, the most useful part of these was the side with the subway maps on it. Like most big cities, the space is much easier to fathom underground. Underground, you can only

---

[4] At the Toronto Festival of Authors, I attended a panel discussion on the topic of "*Publishing in the Zeitgeist.*" about how to publish cutting edge books on contemporary issues. The overriding conclusion was that you can't. By the time a book is written, acquired, edited, produced, and marketed, the zeitgeist will have changed.

go where the trains go. On the surface, there are *options.* Options make things more complicated.

The opposite side of the little folded map, with the streets and streetcar stops marked, was virtually incomprehensible to me. I could plan my routes happily while lying on the bunk in the hostel, but I lack the ability to extrapolate from what I see on a map to what could be in front of me when I step outside the building. It is not until I am actually on the street reading signposts that any of it makes sense.

This is where Google Maps became crucial. A map that I could contain in my phone screen, attach to my bike handlebars, that has a robot voice telling me off when I went wrong and, crucially, that *moves with me* proved essential. Google Maps is an odd phenomenon; instead of relying on physical cues to orientate myself in the real world, I put my blind faith in the digital prompts and expect the physical world to comply and conform to what the screen tells me. On the few times I did get completely lost, I was more frustrated that the city did not look like what was on my screen. It rarely occurred to me that Google could be wrong! This reliance on technology may well kill what little natural orientation skills I have left. Worse, it gives Google an immense amount of power and influence over how we view our world.

I am not entirely comfortable with allowing Google that much control over my movements, and so I have tried to combat this by creating my own maps, included at the end of this book. What mine lack in scale and accuracy, I make up for in enthusiasm and the application of experience. Those maps, and this book are my version of artistically writing the world – or at least, the Torontonian part of it. I made sure to include Graffiti Alley, the dinosaur, and the couch monster, naturally.

Just my Type

I should not have gone to Type.

Not because it is not an excellent bookstore. If anything, it is the most familiar and the most appealing 'type' of bookstore I'd come across in my wanderings. It is a general interest store, unlike the genre-specific places I'd previously found. It was crammed with fascinating titles and haphazard shelving; cosy and compact – no sleek minimalism here. All the books were new, too. Their window proudly displayed a similar line up of bestsellers and new releases to what I have in my own store in Regina. What they lacked in local titles, they more than made up for with diverse authors. I loved it!

There are three branches of Type Books in Toronto, all

in the west of the city. Yet after two days of bookstore hunting, I'd still managed to miss all three of them. I include this Type in the 'South' section because it was the furthest south I could get to in the circumstances.

I should have stopped my journey at The Monkey Paw Bookshop, three kilometres north. I was already exhausted, having walked for five hours already at that point. But, it was only 4pm. I had not found a single copy of *Stroll*; neither had I completed my list of indie bookstores. And I still had another five hours before my flight home. I checked the map and it looked as though, if I walked along Bloor Street to Ossington Station, I could get a bus straight down to within what I took to be a few blocks from Type on Queen Street West. Besides, the friendly goth bookseller in the previous store had told me she used to work at Type. I needed to see it.

The walk to Ossington Station was painful enough. My book bag was heavy now that it was so full, and the thin stringy straps dug into my shoulder uncomfortably. My feet were tired and aching in my unforgiving heels. I sat on the bus gratefully, and…spaced out, staring out the window as the light began to dim in the evening.

Someone pushed past me to get off the bus, and I woke up and panicked. I'd gone too far! I only meant to ride 8 stops. I frantically rang the bell and leapt off. I was at Dundas Street. Good, I recognized that one. I couldn't be too far…north. Realisation hit me like a cold smack from a wet fish. I'd gotten off the bus two stops too early, and now I had even further to walk.

Worse, 'a few blocks' from the bus route on Queen turned out to be eight blocks, and I had inadvertently now made it ten. Ten blocks of pretentious coffee shops and juice bars, sushi restaurants just beginning to open for the evening, and the sort of boutiques with names like 'Tusk' and 'Fawn' that have beautiful window displays but give the casual passer-by no hint as to what lies inside. There were no transit routes along this strip. Then it began to rain.

I decided that journeying back to the hostel in defeat now that I was already wet and miserable would be worse than staggering onward. On the corner of Queen Street West, I noticed another expensive-looking place called 'Bar Poet.' They appeared to be doing a better trade in pizza and wine than poetry, but I took the name to be a sign that I should continue my literary voyage. I am convinced that optimism will be the death of me one day.

Soon the boutiques and restaurants petered out and I found myself passing by the bottom of Trinity Bellwoods Park. The southern edge of the park is elegantly fenced with a tall, ornate metal gate in the middle. In any other circumstances, it would have been the perfect spot to rest on a bench, maybe read a book, or admire this vast expanse of unexpected greenery in the middle of the city. But that day, I was tired to the point of grouchiness. The greenery was still partially frozen, and the rain was rapidly turning to snow. I glared at the gate as I passed, but I carried on. I was convinced I could see Type now!

I was right – Type bookstore is diagonally opposite the south-eastern tip of Trinity Bellwoods Park. I breathed an exhausted sigh of relief and crossed the road.

By now, I had almost developed a script for bookstore introductions, but as soon as the friendly bookseller asked me how I was doing, I blurted out 'knackered!' which must have startled him somewhat, especially since I was dripping rainwater all over his tidy store. I quickly explained the reason for my knackeredness, and the bookseller was impressed. "HOW many did you walk to?" he asked, incredulously. I still don't think he believed me when I told him.

He did not have a copy of *Stroll*, but he did have many interesting sections in his store, including a Staff Picks section so eclectic that I hadn't heard of a single title in it. There were also lots of bookish gifts – stationery, bookmarks, art prints, coffee mugs, and so on and even some Type branded t-shirts. I was tempted, but I felt I couldn't favour this bookstore over any of the others.

The area that attracted me most, however, was the large children's section at the back of the store. It occurred to me that in the previous fourteen bookstores I'd visited, none of them had much geared towards kids. I felt a momentary pang of homesickness, borne of exhaustion. I missed my daft offspring, even though my eldest had texted me at 10pm the previous night, to ask me how to work the tumble dryer. He made the assumption that his father wouldn't know and so felt justified in bugging Mum 2,600 kilometres away. Then my daughter had stolen his phone and I turned mine on that morning to hundreds of crying emojis because I hadn't answered her instantly. She would probably appreciate a little present from my trip, I thought, especially since I'd already bought Milo a book elsewhere.

I couldn't choose a book for her, however. I was slightly proud to find that she already possessed most of the books on Type's main display. I made the decision that she didn't need any more stuffies (although the choice of cuddly animals at Type was impressive). Instead, I settled on a small rubber 'collectible' Bluey squishy in a neat gift box. In the absence of better ideas, Bluey the little Australian dog has universal appeal, and at least this thing would easily fit in my bag.

I apologised to the lone bookseller at the counter for coming all this way to his store and buying toys instead of his lovingly curated books. He shrugged. "Looks like you've already bought plenty!"

Swinging my book bag off my shoulder to unearth my wallet made me appreciate the sheer weight of it properly. He was right – I had bought far too many. Especially for someone who owns a bookstore. I shook my head. Why do I do these things to myself? I had no desire to pick up that bag again, nor to force my aching legs to start walking back to the hostel. The bookseller was hoping to close soon though. I knew this as I saw him beginning to do the dance familiar to everyone who works in retail. There's the subtle closing of the laptop, the neatening of things on the countertop, the gentle straightening of books on the shelf behind him. To the uninitiated, these all appeared innocent, but to weary retail workers everywhere, these are unspoken signs that mean "I hope you leave soon." I took the hint, and reluctantly turned to go. The bookseller shook my hand as I said goodbye, wishing me luck in the bookstore business. I was getting quite accustomed to the sentiment.

How I dragged my sorry-self back to the hostel afterwards, I will never know, but I made it with enough time to sink into the squashy ancient sofa in the basement common area. I checked my phone on Google maps one last time. I had walked 18 kilometres that day. Wincing, I removed my now-hated shoes. I wondered how far towards the airport I could get on TTC if I tried travelling barefoot.

My hostel companions of the previous day had all been replaced during my voyage, and I now found myself sitting with a guy from Manchester. He had only just arrived in Canada, and the hostel staff's jokes about his 'Coronation Street' accent had not gone down well. His response was to ignore them and relax in that traditional British pastime of watching Manchester City football team get utterly defeated on the sports channel on the hostel's giant TV. This was the one and only time during my trip that I actually felt at home. I was as confused by, and as uninterested in English football as the Canadians were. I felt kinship with them, and acceptance.

And I did not want to go home.

Books bought: 0 – replaced by Squishy Bluey
Copies of *Stroll* found: 0
Coffees consumed: 0 – replaced with beer

Part 2: West

Kensington

It is a truth universally acknowledged that hostel coffee must be terrible.

In my experience, the only places in the world where hostel coffee is not terrible are in Central America, where the hostels I stayed in were on working coffee farms.

In urban Toronto, some 6,000 miles north of the equatorial coffee belt, I am met with tepid sad brown liquid. At hostel #1 on the east side of the city, there may have been a motive for the awfulness of the hostel-basement-kitchen coffee. The free – or at least, included – coffee was bad enough to make even the most frugal of student backpackers willing to pay $4 for substantially improved coffee in the official hostel cafe on the main floor.

I crawled down to the basement after a sleepless night in a shared dormitory there. The combination of the terrible coffee and the sight of a shoeless and hairy-toed Dutch guy seemingly guarding the cereal boxes from hungry backpackers, was enough to make me embrace my relative adulthood. I marched to the cafe and purposefully spent $10 on a palatable breakfast. I even felt proud of myself for doing so.

The offerings at hostel #2 on the west side in the Kensington Market area were much better, at least in terms of food. Again, the kitchen was in the basement, and again, the coffee was not wonderful. But this time, it was not to incentivise paying top dollar for espresso in an attached cafe. It just tasted like 'inside of old coffee machine'.

Spontaneously, I invited a hostel buddy to venture down the street with me to Manic Coffee. He was a former Torontonian and in the process of moving back to the city after a stint in the

US, so I hoped he could help me orientate myself a little. It was early, and the guy was only marginally more awake than I was and so the irony of the cafe's name was not lost on either of us. To my surprise, he decided to buy me my favourite Americano, and we sat down together towards the back of the cafe.

"You didn't say thanks," he complained.

I was sure that I had, but I muttered, "Coffee first, then manners."

This elicited a glare as I sipped it.

"Thanks!" I grinned, sheepishly.

As our conversation became more awkward and stilted, I couldn't help focusing on the livelier chatter happening at the table next to us. Two women, a little older than me, were sharing a huge pain au chocolate and discussing 'the characterisation of the female lead.' Little bleeps went off in my head as my ever-present literature-antennae tuned into their discussion. The usual topic of 'impostor syndrome' came up. Then a debate about whether or not it was obvious that 'she' was an unreliable narrator, and how one thought they should introduce the love interest a bit earlier.

WRITERS!

They are Everywhere.

I had tried to explain my bookish obsessions to my hostel companion already, and so I gave him a knowing look towards these women. He was oblivious. Or perhaps he was just more polite about listening in on other people's conversations than I am. I didn't catch much more of their discussion besides a brief disagreement about the difference between 'contemporary fiction' and 'chic lit,' but it was oddly reassuring that, even by accident, I can still find literary types in the wild.

It was becoming clear that my hostel buddy was itching to leave. "Where are you heading?" he asked.

I shrugged. Anywhere. Nowhere. Everywhere. Today was going to be my day for exploration. But it needed to be on foot, and I needed to be alone. We finished our coffees quickly.

I also felt inspired. A book called *Denison Avenue* (by Christina Wong and Daniel Innes) had just been long-listed for the 2024 CBC Canada Reads competition. The book had made me cry. It is all about grief and nostalgia in the face of a rapidly changing community. It is set right here in Kensington Market and the Chinatown area, amidst its gentrification. I was convinced I'd seen the top of Denison Avenue when I walked to the hostel the night before.

"Oh yeah, I think I used to play table tennis on Denison," said my companion as he made a swift exit. That settled it; it felt like as good a place as any to start my voyage.

I had chosen that particular hostel for budget reasons rather than location, but by happy accident, it turned out to be ideal. Kensington Market is certainly turning into a very touristy area (made obvious not only by the hostel's existence, but by the pricier coffee shops like the one we were sitting in), but I still found lots to love. Tiny restaurants were everywhere, with every type of food I could imagine – and some things I had never tried. The Dim Sum houses from Chinatown were still plentiful, but they were interspersed with curry restaurants, shawarma kebab places, and of course, ubiquitous pizza. Then there were the vintage clothes shops: the sort of places where I would wear everything they stock if I could only fit into it, which I usually can't.

The hostel proved to be a great place in which to meet other explorers as well, and I let myself be talked into many Kensington Market excursions. A woman from Brazil, Paola, convinced me that my sentimental desire for a new tattoo commemorating my bookish adventures should be acted upon immediately, and she led me to Inky Dinky Tattoos around the corner from the hostel where I gleefully got inked. Denis the Dutchman introduced me to an icecream parlour that had chipotle flavour cornettos. Later, I met another British woman, Elle, and we saw a band from Montreal playing Leonard Cohen covers on electric fiddles. The spontaneity of the budget backpacker experience is something I hadn't realized I'd missed from my twenties!

My first bookstore-hunting day was overcast and chilly, but the neighbourhood still appeared bright and inviting. Colourful graffiti murals lined many alleys, and posters for every possible event (including a 'candy bra making workshop') fluttered against the streetlights and telephone poles. There were bicycles everywhere locked to bike racks, or often just leaned against the store fronts, carefree. On Augusta Avenue, I found a bar deliberately decorated with sawn up shopping carts. Opposite it was an ancient car spray painted in neon hues, with plants growing out of its roof.

It was only when I began to orientate myself in relation to my list of places I wanted to visit that I realised I was in indie bookstore heaven. There were no less than fifteen of them within a walk of the hostel. That did not include the plethora of comic bookstores and the record shops that often stocked books as well. Getting to fifteen bookstores in one day on foot would prove a challenge, but I was confident it could be done.

I had withdrawn $200 in cash as my 'souvenir' budget for the trip. I knew I would never be able to resist buying things if I was to visit so many bookstores, and the point of this mission was to support the industry, after all. I would limit it to one book per store, I promised myself naively. Unless they stocked *Stroll*, of course. Armed with optimism, my book bag, and my Presto card, I set out.

The Future is Wet

I often feel that big cities lend themselves to science fiction. Something about the 'vertical living' of high-rise apartment blocks still feels futuristic, as if the city itself is reaching for the stars. The seething mass of humanity beneath makes a perfect backdrop for a good dystopia. A city reminds us of what we're good at: exploration and adaptation to different geographies – and what we're pretty terrible at: living together in harmony and balance. If humanity can survive for a few more centuries without succumbing to a self-inflicted apocalypse, it's likely we will do so in megacities.

When sci-fi authors imagine futuristic urban dystopias, they rarely depict places that look like Regina. Toronto, however, seems a more plausible setting. It is already the fourth largest city in North America. The greater Toronto area is home to 6.4 million people. It is not too much of a stretch to believe that in the not-too-distant future, this could be a hi-tech metropolis, complete with flying cars (electric, of course) and soaring skyscrapers that long ago dwarfed the CN Tower.

Professor Megan Smith at the University of British Colombia has produced some bleak and disturbing images of Future-Toronto in her Critical Future Studio project. Together with water engineer Bahman Fakouri, Smith used MidJourney AI to model how Toronto may look in 2054, based on climate data and geographical information from the City of Toronto itself. While this is not necessarily an accurate outcome, the AI compiled prediction is certainly convincing. In the next 30 years, Toronto's maximum daily rainfall is expected to more than double, rising to 166 millimetres from 66 millimetres at present. The risks associated with extreme rain are fairly obvious: they include flooding and damage to public property such as roadways, parks, and ravines as well as private housing; disruption of transit systems and public utilities, and power outages that could devastate city-wide transportation, sewer and water systems. The outlook is bleak. Smith's AI images show the CN Tower standing in a newly formed lake, with flooded and half-destroyed shorter buildings all around.

It rained, and sometimes snowed throughout two of my three trips to Toronto. The weather was an unwelcome surprise to me. Saskatchewan is infamous for its grim, brutal, and extremely long winters. In Regina, it regularly reaches -40°C and the snow lasts from October until April or May. But very rarely does it rain. At most, we get about a week of rain all year, usually in the spring. Hailing from the UK, the year-round sunshine in Saskatchewan is a source of intense joy for me. Toronto's climate feels much more like the cloudy greyness of Northern England that I thought I'd escaped. As such, I can definitely believe Professor Smith's worrying predictions for a catastrophically wet city centre. Her work is definitely based in science, but sadly not all that fictional.

I am somewhat of a sci-fi fan, although I usually favour speculative series. As I am eternally optimistic, I prefer more utopian versions of the future than most modern sci-fi sagas envision. Part of my mission on this excursion was to discuss the future of independent bookstores and to see how other business owners were fairing. I hoped their future looked bright. Where better to begin then, than at a store that specialised in science fiction?

Despite the January melancholy, the residential streets heading north off Spadina Avenue were very pretty. It was also the least futuristic-looking area that I'd explored so far. Gone were the

glass and steel tower blocks of the financial district. The iconic 'flying saucer' shape of the CN Tower was only just visible on the horizon. As I neared the Harbord neighbourhood, the buildings became shorter and older. Delightfully, many of the houses had hand-built Little Free Libraries outside of them. One was even shaped like a spaceship. Soon there were more trees than traffic lights. To my delight, there was also a plethora of bookstores.

Bakka-Phoenix had a great window display: a dizzying array of new science fiction and fantasy novels surrounded a colourful sign saying "New Year, New Dragons." As I am always in the market for a new dragon, I stepped inside. It was not the dragon-themed volumes that caught my eye though. Within a few seconds I'd spied the latest sci-fi anthology from author Elly Blue.

Her books of short stories occupy a subsection of the genre that is niche even to the most fervent of science fiction fans: futuristic speculative stories that involve bicycles. I already owned *Biketopia,* but Bakka-Phoenix had a pile of copies of her latest publication. It is titled *The Bicyclist's Guide to the Galaxy: Feminist, Fantastical Tales of Books and Bikes*. Books, bikes, and a nod to Douglas Adams? This book could have been written just for me!

Resisting the urge to spend all morning in the store, I quickly walked to the counter before I found too many more treasures. The man behind the counter was surprised I had cash; a refrain I heard often during the trip. In that store I suspected I should be using some sort of cryptocurrency, or possibly resorting to a barter system in this post-apocalyptic dystopia. I asked how the business was doing. He shrugged.

"We're still here," he said. "There's always going to be new editions, and we serve a lot of serious collectors." He then told me the store had started a Frequent Buyer program to encourage sales during the pandemic, and asked if I wanted to join. I explained that I didn't live in Toronto so probably wouldn't be able to use it.

"Oh well, no one is perfect," he retorted.

The rain was easing off as I stepped back outside. I looked up again at the sign above the shop and realised I hadn't asked the man the meaning of 'Bakka-Phoenix.' Intrigued, I decided to look it up as soon as I was somewhere dry. The Phoenix part is easily understood – the mythical creature that rises from a fire. The store's website explains that 'Bakka' comes from the Freman language in Frank Herbert's epic *Dune* series. The 'Bakka' is one who weeps and mourns for all mankind.

Much of the *Dune* saga is set on a desert planet, Arrakis,

which is mined for the valuable resource known as 'spice.' This fictional environment could not be further removed from the soggy January morning I was enduring in Toronto, and this is why I enjoy science fiction: it can be pure escapism. Frank Herbert used a lot of Middle Eastern mythology throughout the *Dune* books (although this is missing entirely from the recent movies). Bakka is also an Arabic word meaning 'to crowd,' as in a busy bazaar.

Bakka-Phoenix: this bookstore is a crowded place, rising from the 'flames' of the pandemic whilst weeping for humanity. I cannot think of a more perfect image to sum up the science fiction genre.

Books bought: 1
Copies of *Stroll* found: 0
Coffees consumed: 0

Bibliotherapy

Since opening my bookstore, I have come across many people who describe their books as 'therapy.' They find solace in books. Fictional stories where the characters are relatable teach us that we are not alone. If that familiar character then overcomes their narrative obstacle, it can boost our own confidence too. One of my favourite quotes on the power of stories comes from G.K. Chesterton:

> *"Fairy tales are more than true: not because they tell us that dragons exist, but because they tell us that dragons*

can be slain."

Conversely, reading fiction where the characters are very different to the reader, or when the character has a vastly different opinion to our own, can help us see situations from another perspective. In this sense, reading teaches us empathy and is invaluable. Nonfiction does the same, if less subtly. I firmly believe that a good bookstore should contain something that challenges everyone. Learning to appreciate another's viewpoint is often therapeutic.

I do not consciously turn to books as therapy. However, they do provide me with a form of escapism, which at times is as helpful as therapy and considerably less expensive and intimidating. Immersing myself in another world, even a fictional one, helps me get out of my own head, and that can occasionally do wonders for my mental health. Reading plenty of fiction was invaluable during the pandemic lockdowns, as American aphorist Mason Cooley pointed out:

"Reading gives us someplace to go when we have to stay where we are."

My books certainly helped me through those periods of intense isolation – and in fact, the bookstore was birthed during COVID-19 – but I am still glad to have regained my ability to travel and sometimes escape my home for real. A year or so post-pandemic, and I am free to choose a more literal form of escapism rather than a literary one when the need arises.

Escapism is only ever a temporary fix. I know this; a change of scenery does nothing to actually solve whatever problems are stressing me out. But escapism in this form is always healthier than other intoxicating alternatives. I remain convinced that trips away, however brief, do wonders for my mental health. They allow me to 'reset' a little and re-focus. I also know that the real solution to long term mental wellbeing is to build a life that I don't want to escape from. But that is unrealistic and too far-fetched, even for a fiction lover. No one starts a business if they truly believe it will fail, although the thought of that possibility is never far from your mind. No one starts out wanting to burn themselves out with stress. No one intends to end up impossibly indebted. Yet despite my best efforts this was the exact situation I found myself in at the dawn of 2024. Toronto beckoned, and I ran to it, again. I wasn't running away, I told myself. I was taking a much-needed break.

Little wonder then, that my journeys around Toronto's bookstores eventually led me to Caversham Books, billed as "North America's largest mental health bookstore." It was on the next block west of the Bakka-Phoenix Sci-Fi store; two different forms of bibliotherapy that were neighbours. Perfect! Outside Caversham Books was a little wooden bench painted a cheerful red. Carved in the back of it were the words:

"We are poor indeed if we are only sane"
\- D.W. Winnicott

I didn't recognise the quote, or its author, but I immediately felt that I would like the bookstore. Sometimes, sanity is overrated.

Caversham has been around since 1989 and offered textbooks for schools and library programs. Its biggest attraction is the meticulously curated reading lists on different mental health topics that they publish online for interested groups. Inside the store was an overwhelming mass of overstuffed shelves, but on closer inspection, I found that the books were organised into vague sections and it wasn't as hard to navigate as it first appeared. The vast majority of the books were academic or hard science, inaccessible to the layman like me. I thought again of Milo's ambitions in the field of psychology; maybe he'd become a regular customer here in a few years' time?

Most sections began with 'Psych-': psychoanalysis, psychiatry, psychology, psychotherapy…I checked them all hopefully. This must be the place… but alas, no. There was no psychogeography section. No copies of *Stroll* to be found.

Instead, the Philosophy section caught my eye, because it was folded into a corner behind the extensive Self Help section, which amused me greatly. I thought of a friend who would argue passionately that studying philosophy is one of the worst things you can do for your mental health. Scanning the shelves with him in mind, it was a relief to see only a few books on nihilism. I do wonder if this is a case of correlation being confused with causation: does philosophy make you depressed? Or do depressive people choose to study philosophy?

Rather reluctantly, I moved on to Self Help. I am usually highly cynical about generalised self help books, particularly those written by self-acclaimed 'life coaches.' I doubt that anyone truly has their life together well enough that they can, with any degree of plausibility, teach anyone else their secrets. This is especially true of 'business gurus.' The more time I spend among entrepreneurs and the small business community, the more I realise we are all just making it up as we go along, learning as we go and taking wild guesses. No one knows if they are doing the right thing until they've done it. Instead, we mask our anxiety, focus intently on our goals at the expense of our immediate surroundings, and turn stress into a badge of honour. We love our businesses passionately, will them to succeed, and celebrate small successes when they come. But we would be foolish to think any of us have all the answers.

The two booksellers behind the counter at Caversham Books were no exception to this hyper-fixated mindset. Far from being pushy salesmen, they seemed reluctant to sell me anything at all, so intent were they on their cataloguing and curating. Both men were hunched over desktop computers with filled spreadsheets open on the screen. I had to stand awkwardly waving my book choice at them for a few minutes before the older of the pair deigned to serve me.

I had picked a book that I hoped would be very good for my mental health that was in the 'general interest' section. It was a slim volume called *50 Ways to Protect Bookstores* by Danny Caine. In my (admittedly biased) view, protecting bookstores is good for everyone's mental health, not just that of the indie bookstore owners. Whether it's the wealth of knowledge about our psyches that could be found in Caversham Books, or the escapism of the fantastical futuristic worlds of the sci-fi bookstore beside it, books do become therapy, and we could all use a little therapy from time to time. Neither purchasing that one single book or taking this one little trip away from Regina solved any of my stress or mental health issues, but the knowledge that places like Caversham Books exist certainly helps.

Books bought: 1
Copies of *Stroll* found: 0
Coffees consumed: 0

Little Ghosts

My bookstore in Regina is on the ground floor of a building that houses three businesses. Over the years, we have come to believe the building is haunted. Specifically our space though, and not the adjoining businesses. The ghost only seems to like us.

Our immediate neighbours sell succulents and houseplants. We are divided by thin drywall inside and share a meagre shop 'frontage' outside. As a result, customers are often confused when they walk into a hot and humid plant store when they're expecting a dusty bookshop or visit us only to find *books about* plants rather than living specimens. The plant store owner routinely complained about my neglected and sad-looking snake plant in our window, claiming it was off-putting for her customers. As I felt more than a little ashamed about my lack of green-fingers, I eventually replaced the plant with a fake (crocheted) version. Now, 'the plant lady' and I just exchange mis-delivered mail on occasion and have little other contact.

Far more entertaining are our upstairs neighbours – the yoga studio, run by the building owners, our landlords. Not only are the yogis friendly and outgoing, their clients come downstairs after their classes relaxed and often looking to curl up with a good book after all their exercise. We sell a great many books with mandalas on the cover as a result. However, it is the yoga itself that causes the most amusement. The building is old and creaky, and the walls and ceiling are fairly thin. As a result, we hear almost the entire schedule of the yoga classes in the bookstore, and none of it sounds very zen. Rarely can we tell if it's the floorboards creaking or the knees of the seniors' class. There is a great deal of panpipe music and whale song. The meditational drum circles took us by surprise at first. Other times, there's a noise that sounds a little like Inuit throat-singing, but I'm told it's just breathing exercises. Once a week, there is something that involves large inflatable balls being bounced on the floor very slowly.

I don't know much about yoga, but having grown accustomed to these sounds, none of them cause much alarm anymore. That was until the noises from upstairs grew weirder and much less chilled.

One Saturday, in the early afternoon when the bookstore was at its busiest, there were more incriminating sounds coming through the ceiling. Repetitive squeaking and banging like furniture hitting the walls, random squeals and gasps, and a lot of thumping on the floor. My store manager texted me:

"Sorry to bother you but I think there's an orgy happening upstairs and it's making our customers uncomfortable."

I quickly called the yoga instructor, Colin, asking what on earth was going on above us. His reply was chilling:

"We don't have any classes on Saturday afternoons."

My store manager responded by sending a video recording the noise, and with the ceiling visibly shaking. Colin was as confused as we were, but a whole lot more embarrassed. He curtly said he'd look into it and that was all. After a while, my store manager reported that she'd heard a great many people coming down the stairs, and overheard bits of conversation that included "that was awesome!" and "I'm so glad you had fun, darling."

The mystery was solved the following week, when the noises started up again. Colin rather awkwardly explained that his wife had hired out their yoga studio space without telling him. The noises came from… a children's martial arts session. A dozen eight-year-olds pushing each other over on mats and beating each other up. The revelation was almost disappointing.

But the mysterious orgy was not the only strange happening in the store. Sometimes, the bathroom door refuses to stay closed despite having a lock on the door handle. Occasionally, the front door sounds like it's opening, just a crack, but there's no one there. Post-It notes end up everywhere, but usually nowhere near my desk. All my Sharpie markers disappear. The 'Bookstore' sign hanging over our deck has been maliciously destroyed on three separate occasions. And then, there's the books that inexplicably leap off the shelf at customers.

All these phenomena can be at least partially explained by a combination of the old building and the prairie weather extremes (high winds and often building subsidence, too) and my own absent-minded untidiness. But I can't explain why the books randomly fall off the shelves at people. When that happens, we jokingly blame 'the bookstore ghost,' and assure the customer that the ghost is recommending that title to them. More people are convinced by this than I am comfortable with.

Bookstores invite ghosts, somehow, particularly used bookstores, or classic literature. When you read a classic novel, it is a way of hearing the voice, the ideas, and thoughts of a long dead author, whispering to you from beyond the grave. What's more, you can receive those messages by studying tattoos on pieces of dead tree. Reading is pretty Goth, in some respects.

On my list of bookstores to visit in Toronto was a place called Little Ghosts. Another store with a ghostly incumbent maybe? I was looking forward to this one purely because of the name. It did not disappoint. It did, however, take a long time to get

to on foot. Walking down from Bloor Street and heading further west, I had intended to walk in a loop and end up back somewhere near the hostel in Kensington. It turned out that 'loop' in this case translated to 'walking three sides round a square because I don't know which way is west.' There was a much shorter, easier route I could have taken, but then if I had, I wouldn't have found a cafe that sold 'tortilla bricks' (think: square burritos) for lunch. Afterwards, energised and comfortably full of refried beans, the stroll to Little Ghosts did not seem so far at all.

Little Ghosts is a queer-owned indie bookstore specialising in horror and supernatural books. The store was small and immaculately laid out – considerably less cluttered than my own possibly-haunted business. These were obviously amiable ghosts and not poltergeists. Small fabric ghosts adored the windows and hung from the shelves. A chalkboard outside claimed this was 'Godzilla's favourite bookstore.' The young bookseller inside was entirely dressed in black and white and seemed to fit his surroundings perfectly. To my delight, Little Ghosts also serves coffee. This was definitely my sort of place.

I don't usually read a lot of horror but I do enjoy creepy ghost stories. I scooted past things that looked particularly gory, but noticed all the *Five Nights At Freddy's* graphic novels that my kids love. There were also story collections with titles like *101 Horror Books to Read Before You're Murdered* and *Welcome to Hell: please keep reading*. They also had greeting cards: "Congrats on not dying." There were quite a few queer books on display, trans pride pins for sale at the counter, and one of the ghosts hanging above me was waving a rainbow flag. I am always interested to see the overlap between the LGBTQ2S+ community and geeky book lovers because it is apparent in almost every indie bookstore I know of. In Little Ghosts, the overlap was definitely in the affinity for very dark humour. I loved it.

Floating shelves covered one wall, and the bookseller explained proudly that the books on display there were ones that Little Ghosts had published in house. They were all short story anthologies with distinct themes. He tried to sell me one called *Your Flight Has Been Cancelled* – a collection of horror stories about plane crashes. Given I was flying out of Toronto that evening, I politely declined that one. The idea of a bookstore publishing their own books inspired me, though, even if the subject matter didn't.

I thanked the bookseller for showing me around and invited him to come visit my store if he ever found himself in the prairies. Maybe my bookstore ghost would recommend something good for him. Unable to resist, I bought little glow-in-the-dark ghost stickers and cute bookmarks, and left feeling like I'd made a friend. Little Ghosts was definitely more Casper-esque than *The Turn of the Screw*, but I was certainly filled with good spirits after my visit. A bookstore-publisher was inspirational, and their success in such a niche market was exceptionally encouraging. The world of bookstores welcomes everyone – even, apparently, the undead.

Books Bought: 0, instead: stickers
Copies of *Stroll* found: 0
Coffees consumed: 1 large americano

Used, but not Used Up.

I never have just a 'passing interest' in anything. Once something captures my attention, I let it utterly consume me. When I first started venturing into the bookselling world, I was still obsessing over the minutiae of espresso extraction techniques and roast profiles in my coffee shop. My two passions hadn't quite aligned yet, although I was beginning to see the potential for crossovers.

One element that I think led to the eventual demise of my coffee shop was the sheer size of the building we were in. It was long and huge and entirely open plan. At first it had seemed a great deal to be able to rent somewhere so large relatively cheaply, but soon the size turned out to be a disadvantage. No matter how many people came in or how we spaced the tables, the coffee shop never looked full or busy. It seemed intimidating to customers to come in and sit alone in such a big open space.

Psychogeographically, humans tend not to like open spaces for lengthy periods of time. It's probably a hangover from our time spent avoiding predators in the African savannah. Unless we are in a crowd, we feel too exposed and vulnerable. Take a look at any public park or city plaza: all the benches are located around the edge, looking into the middle of the space. Or they are sheltered beneath trees or around man-made structures like statues or playgrounds. No one ever sits right in the middle on their own. The same phenomenon transpired in my coffee shop; despite the abundance of free space, my customers routinely congregated at the front near the door, or at the bench seating along one wall where the plug sockets for laptops were. Few people ever sat in the middle of the cafe.

My solution to this was to try and break up the space, to give coffee drinkers more structure to huddle around, and make the place seem less empty and intimidatingly sparse. And this, I soon found, was the perfect opportunity to start bringing books into my store. Thanks to my business partner's sharp eyes, we found an enormous, free standing and double-sided shelving unit on a local online marketplace.[5] It was five feet high and seven feet long, and apart from being a bit shabby, it made the perfect, practical room divider. It held a lot of books, too. I put out a call on social media asking for donations of old books. The response was overwhelming.

Soon enough, we had almost filled the shelf. Our new-to-us book collection ranged considerably from an inexplicable number of Dan Brown novels and a well-thumbed copy of *Justine* by the Marquis de Sade, to nonfiction hardbacks on art history donated by my partner's girlfriend's mother. I feel this says a lot about Regina.

This first foray into the book world wasn't strictly commerce. Our collection on the giant shelf was a book *exchange*. If people brought books to donate, they could help themselves to anything already on the shelf. I believed this was an exchange of ideas in action. Naively, and distracted by my barista duties, I did not monitor exactly what was being exchanged.

I was dimly aware that more people were leaving books than taking them away again, but the new "book seats," the chairs I'd stationed near the bookshelf were at last getting some use. The books were providing a reassuring backdrop to the cafe tables, and I didn't much mind what books they actually were.

---

[5] The site is called UsedRegina.com. That name has caused juvenile sniggering for years in our household.

Unfortunately, a few months in, we came to a "book blockage." There was no more room for donated books, and the book donors did not want to take anything away. The Dan Brown novels had at least found a new home, and someone had tried to pay me real money for some pristine copies of the Twilight Saga in hardcover (I refused it). But the remaining collection consisted almost entirely of Harlequin novels and James Patterson books. These are the things that regularly get donated but rarely get reclaimed. And now I was stuck with them.

This experience left me highly reluctant to ever get back into the world of used books. When I opened The Penny University Bookstore, I was determined to only stock new things. There are other used bookstores in Regina, and I admire the owners' curation abilities, but I had no desire to compete with them. This never stopped hopeful people calling the bookstore asking if I accepted book donations, or occasionally, whether I would *buy* their used books. Our answer was always the same – thanks, but no thanks. I often wonder if selling used books might be a useful extra revenue stream, but then I think back to the final, sad days of my coffee shop. Emptying boxes of beaten-up paperbacks with shirtless men on the covers into a dumpster was far from my proudest moment.

I will continue to leave the used book stock curation to the experts, for they are many. I discovered a concentration of used bookstores around the Kensington Market area of Toronto, all similar in some ways, but unique in others. In stores like mine that sell new, mainstream, and general interest books, I am now fairly adept at guessing what will be on display. It is likely that we all receive the same sales emails from publishers exalting their latest releases. We all scour the same book review sites and read the book columns in the same newspapers. A lot of us subject ourselves to watching 'Booktok' to see what's trending. Used bookstores do not receive the same briefings. Instead, they stock whatever they can get that they want to sell. This allows them to stock highly unique collections, and it gives book lovers the chance to discover previously unknown treasures.

The first of these used bookstores I found was Sellers and Newel. As the name suggested it was run by a pair of men, but I never found out who was Mr. Sellers and who was Mr. Newel. In their extremely full store, I found a copy of Terry Pratchett's *Raising Steam* with a cover that I hadn't seen before. I did have all of Pratchett's Discworld books, but I'd left my original copy of *Raising Steam* in the hospital labour ward when my daughter was born! Nearly nine years later, I was very pleased to finally restore it to my collection.

When I approached the cash desk (tucked right in the back of the store in a sort of alcove), Mr. Sellers (or maybe Mr. Newel) remarked that he was glad I'd found something I wanted, as it wasn't easy stocking series of books in a used bookstore. They knew they would never be able to have all 41 Discworld books in stock at the same time, and it was sheer luck that they had the one book I was missing on that day. This made my find feel even more special. When I explained how I was on a quest to visit as many indie bookstores as I could, Mr. Newel (or possibly Mr. Sellers) looked up from his laptop.

"Oh, are you in the industry?" he asked. I explained that yes I was, but that I focused on new books only.

"Doesn't matter!" he replied. "You're a bookseller. A pleasure to meet you!" He shook my hand and proceeded to knock 20 per cent off the pencilled-in price in the front of the paperback.

"We better give you an industry discount," his partner explained. The discount meant I had enough change left to pay in cash, another thing that they were very pleased about.

***

Next on my list was Balfour Books, on the same street as my hostel, but further west. Balfour sells used, rare, and antiquarian books, but no new ones. Like many of the stores I'd come across already, there was a wooden trolley outside with extremely cheap books in it. I assume these are excess stock; the books much like my Harlequin and James Patterson paperbacks from the coffee shop that just don't go anywhere. I do find it incredibly trusting of store owners to do this, and I often wonder how many people just help themselves without paying. I also get the impression that the store owners don't care much. There is an old adage that sprang to mind: "Thieves don't read, and readers don't thieve."

Balfour's bargain shelf had books marked down to just one dollar. I rifled through and quickly saw one that Theia would love and brought it inside. When I first entered the dimly lit shop, the owner was standing on a rickety stool, trying to wedge a large, old, and very heavy looking hardback into a minute space on the shelf far above his head. It did not look safe at all. I am fairly tall anyway and made more so by my uncomfortable high heels that I was bitterly regretting by this point in my walk. I thought I should at least take advantage of the heels and asked the bookseller if he needed my help. He shook his head furiously.

"Thank you, but no. This edition is worth nearly $2,000. I can't let you touch it I'm afraid."

As he said this, I noticed he was wearing gloves, but the revelation about the book made his stance on the stool seem all the more precarious. Despite having chosen a book already, I browsed around a little, trying not to distract the man or stare too hard, in case I endangered the operation further. Eventually, the man managed to shelve the book, and replaced his stool neatly in the back of the shop. I brought my book up to the counter again, feeling a little sheepish about only spending one dollar when there were books on sale for thousands.

That transaction got me wondering – how does one determine the monetary value of old books? Why was his heavy hardback worth $2,000, when my book about kids with wild imaginations was only $1? Although the presence of the bargain shelf outdoors implied a lack of consumer demand, books are such a subjective thing that there must be more to it. I suspect it is much like the antique trade: there are industry standards for pricing and valuation, only known to the inside few. This is yet another skillset, like the ability to keep track of and curate a marketable collection from hundreds of donations, that I fervently admire in booksellers but have no wish to emulate.

The owner of Balfour Books enthusiastically helped guide me on my quest by mentioning several other stores I should go to. He mentioned Sellers and Newel, and then Little Ghosts, because I "seemed like the type who would like that place." Then he told me that the owner of Little Ghosts complained that many people tried to donate old books to that store, and they in turn passed the would-be donors on to Sellers and Newel. "And if they don't want them, they come here!" he laughed. Even in a big city, the booksellers' network is close-knit it seems.

Having exhausted the possibilities on College Avenue for the time being, I ventured North again to Doug Miller Books, as directed by the man at Balfour. Doug Miller was also owner-operated, and of these three, this was the store that appeared the most disorganised inside. There were books stacked everywhere, with very little sorting or categorising to be seen. Keen booklovers could easily spend hours in there, treasure-hunting. However, this was not the place to look for something specific.

I naively asked the bookseller (I assume, Mr. Miller) if he had a copy of *Stroll*. He looked at me blankly and then shrugged. "Maybe," he managed. "The nonfiction is over there." He gestured vaguely to the opposite wall, and I pretended to search. Some of the nonfiction books were still in cardboard boxes with The Wine Cellar printed on the side. I did not hold out much hope of finding it, even if he did somehow have a copy.

Not really knowing where to start, I again found the bargain shelf, only this time it was tucked just inside the entrance. I chose a dystopian horror about eugenics, just because it looked interesting. I was having an excellent day and so needed a good dose of gritty, depressing futurism to balance it out. But as I went to pay for it, my eye was caught by another stack that had some of Caitlin Moran's books on it, including one I was sure I didn't already own. I tried to swap it.

"Oh, don't worry about it," said Mr. Miller. "Just keep both, I don't mind." So, I paid $5 for two paperbacks and quickly stuffed them in my bag before he could change his mind.

Mr. Miller's generosity and lack of inventory management were not the most unique things about the business. As I browsed the store, it became apparent that the owner is a serious Lego aficionado. Behind the counter, he had a huge collection of Lego minifigures and even more of them in a lit cabinet behind his head. These were perhaps the tidiest areas of the store. At the back, there was an entire archway, tall enough for me to walk through without stooping, entirely made of Lego bricks and with the store's name picked out in red bricks on a white background. Once I had started spotting the Lego, I suddenly saw it everywhere. Right above the bargain shelf was a Lego Christmas Village (even though it was late January by the time I visited). The village was being terrorized by a Lego T-rex. Finally, I realised that the store's counter that I had just been leaning on, was also entirely made of Lego. I asked Mr. Miller if he minded me taking photos. He shook his head, and I took many souvenir pictures for my husband. He is also a Lego fan, but I hoped it wouldn't give him too many ideas.

When I first began this bookstore odyssey, I had contemplated ruling out used bookstores, rudely assuming they would all be the same. I was very glad to be proved wrong in this judgement. Visiting these three distinct used bookstores had been a journey through time and community. Each shop—whether overflowing with well-worn paperbacks, rare first editions, bargains waiting to be rediscovered, or even the Lego—reminded me that books, though used, are never truly used up. Someone, somewhere collects the paperbacks with shirtless men on the covers. James Patterson has many, many fans, I'm sure. But these books carry stories not just within their pages, but also in the hands of all who have held them before, in the conversations they inspire and in the places they inhabit. In a city as vibrant as Toronto, these bookstores serve as quiet, treasured spaces, preserving the past while fuelling the imaginations of today. Who knows, maybe it is time I brought a shelf of used books into my store at long last!

Books bought: 4
Copies of *Stroll* found: 0
Coffees consumed: 0

Flying Across Communities (Another Story About Rain)

After what felt like a very long walk on College Street – but can only have been a few more blocks west of my starting point – was Flying Books. Flying Books has an excellent reputation online and was the first mainstream and new bookstore I'd come across since Type Books. I had hoped that it would at least be slightly like my own store, and as such, I was looking for advice and inspiration there. On a later visit to Toronto, I found a new store called Flying Books at Neverland, down on Queen Street West. This one did not have a huge range of books in it, but it combined book sales with a cocktail bar. This new venture told me that Flying Books is obviously doing something right, and it was exciting to see somewhere so bright, vibrant, and successful.

The original Flying Books store on College Street is laid out in a very minimalist style. There were neat piles of books on tables rather than squashed into free-standing shelves and lots of open space surrounding them. It was a complete contrast to all the used bookstores that I'd come across so far, and for that reason, it was visually appealing.

The woman working that day seemed hurried. She was trying to deal with an enthusiastic man who was determined to get her to stock his own new self-published book. This situation was more than a little familiar to me as we stock a huge number of 'consignment' authors in The Penny University. Over the years, we have learned to tell which of these authors' books will sell, and which will take up shelf space for time immemorial. It is often tricky to balance politeness and encouragement while not giving false hope or unrealistic expectations of sales. It seemed that the Flying Books staff understood this struggle too and had judged this author to be in the latter slow-sales category. I feigned interest in his book to help her out a little. She seemed relieved, and the man beamed. His sales pitch for the book was sleek and impressive and he'd clearly practised this on other bookstore owners. I sincerely hope he found some stockists.

I discovered that Flying Books is also a book publisher and have a small range of their own publications proudly displayed on floating shelves along one wall. Given that fact, I was not entirely sure if they even took books on consignment as the author wished. I promised him I'd buy the book *when* it was available in stores, just in case. I'd hoped that this would be enough to begin a conversation with the bookseller properly. The woman, who I took to be the owner, must have heard me explaining that I was touring bookstores. After commenting that there were 'so many good places nearby,' I think she realised I wasn't likely to be buying much. She didn't stay to chat for long.

I recognised a great many of their books from my own stock and a good number in their 'local' section, too. When you stock authors local to a city like Toronto, you tend to have more well-known authors in it than the same section does in Regina. Flying Books has Catherine Hernandez, Andre Alexis, and Kerry Clare as 'local.' I was beginning to suffer from intense feelings of Small Town Inadequacy. But then another section caught my eye – the Indigenous section. Whilst I am always pleased to see Indigenous-authored books in these stores, I think their placement speaks volumes about Canadian bookstores, and Canada in general. There is a silent, but clearly visible divide; 'local' here is physically separated from 'Indigenous' as if the two are mutually exclusive. Being Indigenous does not exclude you from being local to Toronto. Flying Books is not alone in categorising in this fashion, but the division was made more starkly apparent in a store that was so spaciously laid out.

I eventually chose a book called *Reuniting with Strangers* by Jennilee Austria-Bonifacio from the Local section. It is all about Filipino immigrants to Canada being separated from their families for lengthy periods. Its central theme is exploring what happens when the people you are supposed to be closest to suddenly seem unfamiliar. This was very true of Flying Books – the store most similar to my own bookstore in terms of stock and focus seemed somehow detached and strange. I'd got used to the unabashed weirdness of both my own business and the eccentricities of the other Toronto bookstores I'd visited so far. Seeing a mainstream, general interest store all tidy and neatly arranged and with a somewhat brusque store owner felt quite alien after everything I'd encountered elsewhere.

*****

I was already quite far west of the downtown core by this point so it seemed only logical to continue. I unlocked a new rental bike and stayed on College Street, heading for Roncesvalle. I hoped this neighbourhood is pronounced phonetically because I realised mid-pedal that I'd never heard anyone say it aloud. Ron-sez-val? Roncy-vale? I still don't know. But it was a long way west.

Five minutes after unlocking the bike, the heavens opened.

I had gotten rained on several times in Toronto already, but this was an exceptional downpour. There was no shelter anywhere on my route and I had little choice but to keep going and endure it because I knew turning around was not going to magically dry me off. The rain was so hard that I needed windshield wipers on my glasses. I stopped briefly to take them off and cycled the rest of the way with next to no depth perception. Mercifully, it is quite flat and I did not fall in any pot holes.

I docked the bike a little earlier than I needed to, unsure where the next dock would be. Continuing on foot allowed me to ring water out of my hair and shake at least some of the rain out of my clothes. It was intense, but it was also warm storm rain and the exercise at least kept me at a comfortable temperature. My bag (already loaded up with books) was worryingly damp, however. I was concerned that my new purchases would end up with curly pages before I'd even opened them.

Roncesvalle is pretty, tree-lined, and full of boutique businesses. It actually felt a little like my home community of Cathedral in Regina in that respect, although more multicultural. Sadly, my neighbourhood does not boast Latino bars or Polish bakeries. To my delight, Roncesvalle Avenue is large enough to support two independent bookstores and a branch of the comic book store, 'She Said Boom!' I had come out looking for Another Story Bookstore – a general-interest place that seems to hold a great many book launches and author signings. Their website informed me that they were founded in 1987.

Another Story was not where I thought, however. Instead, still half-blinded by the rain and confused by my lack of glasses, I walked into the first place I could find that looked like a bookstore.

This one turned out to be called A Good Read. For some reason, it had never popped up when I had researched the area, so it was a welcome addition to my journey. I hesitated in the doorway, trying to shake off as much rainwater as I could before entering. I did not want to drip all over their displays. The bookseller inside told me the store was around seventeen years old, still with the original owner. Roncesvalle is obviously an area where small businesses are very long-lived.

A Good Read stocks both new and used books and some rare and collectable ones as well. It also had a fun collection of unusual 'book paraphernalia': book sleeves[6], reading glasses, clip-on book lights, and even bookish t-shirts. Given my damp circumstances, I chose to forego buying even more books in this store and opted for a new book *bag* instead. I ceremoniously dumped out the contents of my soaked tote and replaced them in my new, shiny, and dry one from a company called 'Out of Print.'

The staff at A Good Read were kind enough to tell me that Another Story Books was only one block further south; I hadn't gone too far wrong on my journey. As always, I appreciated the fact that bookstores help each other out far more often than they try to compete.

Another Story Books was absolutely crammed with books, perhaps the biggest new bookstore I'd yet seen. As I walked in, no longer dripping but still dramatically bedraggled, I was greeted with a large display of new releases, including one by S. Bear Bergman – a graphic novelist, Regina resident, and Milo's classmate's dad. The bookish world is a small one indeed.

After my observations about book categories at Flying Books, I had a look around to see how Another Story classified their books. They have New Releases, Bestsellers, a loose division between fiction and nonfiction, and a magnificent children's section. Like in my own store, Indigenous titles were mixed into their respective genres. When I asked, they explained they have a section especially for self-published Torontonian authors and local

---

[6] None of the book sleeves looked waterproof unfortunately – I definitely think there is a market for waterproof book sleeves if my experience of book shopping in the rain is anything to go by.

authors published by small presses, but they don't have a section for traditionally-published authors who just happen to live in Toronto.

"It wouldn't make much sense to do that," the bookseller

said. "It would be too big."

Unfortunately, this meant no copies of *Stroll* were on display. "Isn't there a new one?" the bookseller asked. He did not seem to understand why I was so keen to find the old edition, but suggested I try searching in the used section of A Good Read up the road. This prompted me to ask about the competition and what it was like with a similar store so close by.

"Oh, it's all very friendly," he replied. "If we don't have something, we send people there, and vice versa. It's almost like having two stores."

The store manager appeared happy to talk business, and to my delight, he even had photocopies of an Indie Bookstore Map of Toronto. I explained that I was attempting to create my own, and my explorations in the rain were what had got me so drenched that day. "We've been here nearly forty years," he said kindly. "You are not the most rain-soaked person to come in." I'm not sure if that should tell me more about Toronto's climate or the store's determined clientele.

The rain had not abated, and so after thanking the owner of Another Story for his time, I made my way to a bright yellow cafe across Roncesvalle Avenue, called 'Coffee and All That Jazz.' I spent long enough there to dry out and fueled up with a huge sandwich, then I caught a streetcar back east. The rain was unpleasant, but it was not enough to diminish my resolve. If anything, the west end stores had shown me the wonderful way bookstores create community and that is definitely worth getting wet for. It is not just through their choice of books that highlight so many voices from different communities; it is also in the way they support each other and collaborate rather than compete. In a time of isolation, societal polarization, and economic hardship for customers as well as small businesses, strengthening local communities becomes a radical, beneficial act.

Books bought: 2 - and a bag
Copies of *Stroll* found: 0
Coffees consumed: 1

Part 3: North

BMV and the Curse of the Remaindered

I always knew there'd be one. In fact, I am relieved that there was only one. One bookstore on my list that was closing down, or at least appeared to be.

BMV is a store for bargain books, used books, and in at least one branch, coffee too. I assume it stands for 'Books, Music, Video' and although it had some CDs on display, I think they have now given up on the 'video' sales. I had first come across the small indie chain in 2019 when I fell into their downtown branch on Edward Street. I was seduced by the "Any book: $2" sign above a substantial pile of interesting titles in a bright red cart outside the store. I left with an enormous coffee, a book of coldbrew coffee cocktail recipes, and Mo Willem's *Elephant and Piggy Omnibus* for Theia, and still had change from $20. Even then, prying myself away was difficult. BMV offers the sort of cheap and cheerful, utterly unpretentious shopping experience that I enjoy the most.

'Bargain' books like those at BMV are an odd phenomenon in the indie bookstore world. They occupy a niche in the market that makes books accessible to more people: those without much in the way of disposable income mainly, but also people who don't frequent bookstores. These bargain books are the ones you find at Walmart or Giant Tiger, or inexplicably nestled behind a rack of beach towels in Winners. Their existence allows retailers to buy books without having to declare themselves 'a bookstore' and all the accompanying bureaucracy of dealing with publishers that the status usually involves.

BMV offers what is on their shelves, no more and no less. There is no catalogue of stock on their website, no pre-ordering of new releases and no means of ordering anything that isn't visible when you walk in. This helps keep things simple for the store managers and keeps costs down for customers. The 'hunt' for books in their stores is perhaps what creates BMV's loyal fanbase.

But 'bargain' books like this are maligned in the bookstore industry. For serious booklovers, the cheapness implies that they are low quality, which is rarely the case. Books for sale with big "$5" stickers on them always seem to imply there's something wrong with them. In most instances, however, these bargain books are still brand new in the sense that they have not yet been read. This means the 'quality' in the physical sense is unchanged. They just might be a little beaten up, or shelf worn. ('Shelf worn' is a sweet euphemism for "this gathered dust for many months until someone knocked it off the shelf and bent the corner.") The content inside does not change.

Bargain books are technically called 'remaindered.' That is, when a print run of books is too large, or when bookstore owners are overly optimistic and order in more books than they can sell, and eventually return them to the publisher. If this happens after the book has been in circulation for a while and the buzz about it has worn off, the publisher has an unpleasant choice: either pulp the books and destroy them or attempt to sell them on again as 'remaindered' stock. If they are lucky, selling remainders just about covers the cost of printing the books in the first place, but little else. Either way, these books represent the publisher 'giving up' on that title.

There are a few wholesale companies who buy up remainders and sell them back to bookstores like BMV at impossibly cheap prices. These wholesalers deliberately make it obvious that the books are rendered 'bargains' by adding 'remainder' marks – usually a dab with a Sharpie across the top of the pages, or cutting the corner off the dust jacket. This infuriates book collectors; I have met a few people who were shockingly snobbish about this. Buying a book in pristine condition is a great feeling, but a single Sharpie swipe across the top does not alter the text inside in any way, shape, or form. Instead, you have a book that's never been opened by another human, potentially from a well-known and talented author, at a fraction of the original retail price. What's not to love?

As a business model, it makes a lot of sense. In early 2023, I had attempted to open a second location to my bookstore, named 'Tuppenny,' (to go with the original 'Penny' books, of course). Tuppenny was going to be a bargain bookstore and coffee shop and be used as a venue for all my book launches. I was sure to stock up on the very best of the remaindered books I found at the wholesalers, and flat-rated it all at $10 a book. It would be simple, bargainous, and profitable, or so I thought. It seemed like such a good idea at the time: selling good books with a profit margin of 70 percent or more beats selling perfect books with 40 percent profit. On paper, it looks infallible. Unfortunately, the reality seems to differ.

BMV used to have four branches around Toronto. The first I found was its downtown store, with the coffee bar in it near Dundas Square. There is another a long way north on Yonge near the Eglinton area. And then there was a branch on Queen Street. That one closed in 2020, but its last day was in January – so not a Covid casualty. Finally, there is another BMV on Bloor Street that I attempted to visit on my most recent excursion. It was absolutely enormous – a true book superstore filling several storeys.

But the Bloor Street branch was a sad sight on that day, disheartening for me in many ways. The cafe part was closed on a Thursday morning, when the surrounding area seemed fairly busy. I was in dire need of a coffee at that point. I felt doubly disappointed.

I saw many parallels with my Tuppenny venture. By January 2024, I had hit metaphorical rock bottom: Tuppenny was failing to the point where I couldn't afford to pay my staff, so I'd let them all go and tried to carry on alone, whilst simultaneously trying to run the main bookstore as well as doing all the stocking and marketing and organising all the events at both locations. And work my various volunteer roles as well. As was obvious to everyone else in my life except myself, this was not a sustainable situation. And then, as if I wasn't suffering enough, I had to suddenly repay my CEBA loan as well. Something had to give, and I knew deep down that I had to close Tuppenny. At that point, I just didn't know how to do so. Instead, knowing that I still had to make the rent, I'd opted to cut Tuppenny's opening hours right down to 'just Saturdays'. I could work that without dying of exhaustion, I reasoned. Saturdays were the only day that it was busy enough to make any money. I would be saving money by not paying staff or buying supplies for the rest of the week. It was a dismal solution, but I felt like I had very few options.

The same appeared to be true of the Bloor Street branch of BMV. The opening hours posted on the door of the attached cafe looked as though they'd been cut back and cut back to the bare minimum necessary for the store's survival; in this case, Fridays and Saturdays only. There were huge sale signs in the window "EVERYTHING 3 for $10." I recognised the signs of desperation from bitter experience.

I do not know the fate of that branch of BMV. At the time of writing, a Google search informs me that it is still open, and now has much longer opening hours, so hopefully it overcame whatever difficulties it was facing in January. The same cannot be said of Tuppenny – I was eventually forced to find an entirely separate company and subleased the cafe side of it. It is now mine in name only and looks nothing like the bookstore-cafe I'd envisioned. The sublease was the best possible outcome in the circumstances, but I still feel devastated about it to the point that I'm reluctant even to set foot in the space now.

I can blame my location. I can blame my lack of marketing skills or budget. I can blame the CEBA loan. Most often I blame myself for some form of mismanagement. But truly, I don't know why Tuppenny didn't work out. And I don't know why BMV was on the verge of closing either.

Maybe it's the bargain books. Unloved the first time, shelf-worn and bruised, and then scarred by Sharpies and sold on as if worthless. Maybe bargain books are just cursed and reaping their revenge.

Books bought: 2
Copies of *Stroll* found: 0
Coffees consumed: 1

Caribbean Ekistics and a British Eccentrics

In 2022, British comedian, broadcaster, and scientist Robin Ince published a book titled *Bibliomaniac*. Following the launch of his previous book, Ince embarked on a book tour and tried to visit 100 bookstores in the UK in 100 days. Furthermore, he travelled between them using only public transport. I had heard of Robin Ince via his Infinite Monkey Cage radio show with Professor Brian Cox, and knew him as a scientist first and foremost, albeit a very funny one. I had no idea of his love of books.

For my birthday this year, long after I had begun my own Canadian bookstore odyssey, my parents bought me a copy of *Bibliomaniac*. I enjoyed the book immensely, especially his tales from parts of the UK that I remember fondly. Ince has a knack of occasionally phrasing something so simply that I wonder why I've had so much trouble articulating the same sentiment myself in my own work. For example, when describing a bookstore owner's motivation for opening her own shop, he simply states:

"Bookselling is driven by a desire to inflame a passion for reading."

A good point, well made. (It is then followed by a convoluted tangent about the definition of 'avuncular underwear,' so I cannot take inspiration from everything in this book.) I choose to view the book as confirmation that other people have an interest in the same things I do – a parallel evolution of ideas, if that does not sound too grandiose. However, I was also a little put out that someone had beaten me to it! Particularly as that person is a celebrity!

Most amusingly, and particularly ironically given the next leg of my venture, I discovered my parents had cheaped out. My copy of *Bibliomaniac* has a pencilled dedication in the front.
"70th birthday gift," it reads, "from Emily, Max and Freddy." None of these people are known to my parents, and I am still a long way from 70. The weird world of used books being what it is, it seems likely that Emily, Max or Freddy will one day find *this* book. If they do, and recognise themselves, please know that I appreciated the indirect gift, even if the intended recipient appears to have donated it to a used bookstore somewhere near my parents' home on the Welsh border.

Somehow, I doubt Robin Ince himself will mind that my copy of *Bibliomaniac* is second-hand. His adventures in British used bookstores did resonate when I came across Seekers Books on Bloor Street West. It was everything a used bookstore should be – well stocked, with 'a bit of everything,' crowded with yellowing paperbacks stacked in every available space, knowledgeable staff and, of course, a large ginger cat. Seekers is well named – I had to seek it out, as the store is in a basement unit down some steps from street level. A colourful mural (featuring the cat) leads book lovers down to the treasure trove.

In it, I found another predominantly British-authored book: *The Penguin Book of Cities*, with short stories by some of my literary and geographically-minded heroes: Will Self and Irvine Welsh. When I went to buy it, I started my now-rehearsed speech about finding as many bookstores as I could. The bookseller seemed pleased that someone was visiting so many stores and told me of several others in the surrounding neighbourhood. Much like Kensington Market below us, I seemed to be in the middle of a concentration of stores, all vastly different but with similar missions: to build a community of like-minds and then serve that community with good books. Seekers appeared to attract a particular sort of reserved, introverted and possibly nocturnal clientele, as evidenced by its opening hours: midday to midnight.

My Book of Cities is fictional, but parts of it touch on the same ideas about the way neighbourhoods operate that Robin Ince was expressing in his bookstore tour. I learned a new word from his book: ekistics. Ekistics, in simple terms, is the science of human settlements. I decided this was something I needed to research immediately. More broadly, ekistics is the study of the interplay between nature, human behaviour, society, 'shells' – that is, dwellings and shelters – and the networks that connect them all. So far, so psychogeographical.

I continued my wanderings along Bloor Street with these concepts swirling around in my head. Bloor Street West is a main thoroughfare and the 'corridor' prides itself on being extremely culturally diverse. The ekistics, now that I know what this means, are fascinating. On foot, one element that was immediately noticeable was that all the storefronts are squashed right on the sidewalk. There were very few entrances up steps or with sheltered vestibules, and a lot of the stores had racks of stock on the sidewalk outside. It was also surprisingly green, even in January, with numerous 'pocket parks' dotted on the side streets. Bloor Street West had an abundance of bike lanes and transit stops; elements that I've come to associate with areas inhabited by newcomers to Canada. If you have just arrived - either as an immigrant or as a tourist like myself - then you are less likely to have a car at first. Whether the diverse populations demanded the transit options or whether the transit options led them to this area is much harder to determine.

Bloor Street West blends a mix of residential, commercial, and cultural spaces spanning several neighborhoods, from the student-centric vibe near the University of Toronto to the more upscale shopping districts for neighbourhoods like the Annex and the top of Roncesvalle. As I headed west, I passed through 'Little Korea.' There is also a large Jewish community around there. What I did not know was that the area surrounding Bloor Street and Bathurst is also a Black neighbourhood, founded by Caribbean immigrants and displaced folks who escaped the US via the Underground Railroad.

"In 1842, a Black kid named William Peyton Hubbard was born at Bloor and Brunswick Street, one of 1,000 African Canadians in a Toronto population of 40,000." - *Royson James, Welcome to Blackhurst.*

In 1894, Hubbard became the city's first non-white alderman, won fifteen elections, and served as acting Mayor of

Toronto. He was also instrumental in the creation of the Toronto hydro system.

Bloor and Bathurst is also the home of Contrast newspaper that became the 'eyes, ears and voice of the Black community' after its founding in 1969. Author and memoirist Austin Clarke hailed from the neighbourhood as well, as did Makeda Silvera, the founder of Sister Vision, which was Canada's first Black women's publishing company.

Of course I learned all this in a bookstore. Less than five minutes' walk from Seekers Bookstore, I came across a place named "A Different Booklist," a Black-owned and founded 'multicultural bookstore specialising in books from the African Caribbean Diaspora and the Global South.' Beside it is the 'Different Booklist Cultural Centre' and beside that is a Midas car lot. The CN Tower pokes up above it, and competing for my attention was a bright yellow wacky-waving-inflatable-arm-flailing-tube-man (or an "air tube dancer," for anyone who doesn't watch Family Guy). It seemed to be trying to dance with the CN Tower and I must have stood watching it for several minutes, captivated. Years ago, I learned that air tube dancers had been invented by a carnival artist from Trinidad named Peter Minshall. I have no idea why I retained that piece of information, but it seemed poignant at the time.

As I browsed around A Different Booklist, something unexpectedly caught my eye. Here, at long last, was a copy of Shawn Micallef's *Stroll*! I had almost forgotten this was the reason for my quest. It seemed an unlikely book to stock in such a place. I asked the bookseller about it, and she shrugged. "We just thought it would appeal to people; it's still all about Toronto, isn't it?" she said.

Dear reader, I did not buy *Stroll* that day. Even after going round sixteen other bookstores looking for it. I was in A Different Booklist now, after all, and the purchase did not feel right, somehow. I was distracted by discovering that as well as a bookstore and a cultural centre, I was also inside the home of 'A Different Publisher.' Instead of *Stroll,* I purchased *Welcome to Blackhurst - An Iconic Toronto Neighbourhood*. It is an essay collection published by A Different Publisher and featuring contributions from experts in the local community. There are stories about first arrivals in Canada from the Caribbean, about seeing the first snowflakes landing on the streetcar tracks, about entrepreneurs and creatives and about the jazz clubs and small restaurants that line the edges of Bloor Street West. It is about a community network that has fought for and created a home in a strange and often unwelcoming place.

Until this point, my explorations of Toronto had been largely influenced by *Stroll,* written by a white, middle class academic. The later parts of my bookstore tour took inspiration from Robin Ince's *Bibliomaniac*, another book by another white, middle class academic, and both quite similar to myself. '*Welcome to Blackhurst*' would give me a vastly different perspective on similar topics, and that could only be a good thing, I reasoned. This was definitely the part of my journey that taught me the most, and I got to dance with a giant yellow tube man, too.

Books bought: 2
Copies of *Stroll* found: 1
Coffees consumed - 0.

Drag Brunch

I have really grown to love Toronto. No doubt I wouldn't feel the same if I actually *lived* here, but for an impromptu break every so often, it is perfect. The city is unassuming, welcoming, and full of interesting people. It is also considerably less conservative than most of Western Canada.

More than anything in Toronto, I relish the chance to feel anonymous, but also *bold*. I have now lived in Regina for longer than I've ever lived anywhere before. I do love the sleepy, flat prairie city, and I could not have asked for a better place to raise our kids. I know I would not have been able to grow my small businesses in quite the same way anywhere else. Regina is also small enough that it is easy to become famous — or at least, notorious. Everyone knows each other within certain communities in Regina. The literary and bookish community is small but infinitely supportive. The queer community is even smaller, and the overlap between the two is considerable.

In terms of business, this is sometimes useful. For instance, I rarely have to spend money on advertising. But personally, it is another matter. This 'fame' that comes from being the owner of the only mainstream bookstore in town provides welcome ego-boosts at times of need, but it also fills me with fear. If I fail — which I am doing now both in business and in life in general — then *everybody knows.* There is no hiding place in the fishbowl, and unlike fish, Regina residents' memory is longer than six seconds. I closed my coffee shop venture in 2017 due to monumental failure. To this day, people still refer to me as 'Dr. Coffee.' People *remember* your screw ups in Regina. Forever.

But in Toronto, I am no one.

At the same time, I am also anyone I want to be, without expectations and with fewer inhibitions. I love it.

One Sunday morning, I decided to embrace my no one/anyone big city identity. I donned my favourite purple and green jumpsuit, screwed my hair up into 1990s 'space buns' on top of my head, and took the streetcar to Church Street to the 'Drag Brunch' at Glad Day Bookshop. It was fabulous and exactly what I needed. The area just east of Yonge Street and running north towards Rosedale is Toronto's gay village neighbourhood. I had just caught the tail end of Pride month, too. Rainbows were *everywhere*. I was pleased to see I was not the most colourfully-dressed person wandering up Church Street that morning, although someone did stop me to ask where I'd bought my jumpsuit.

Glad Day Books is the oldest queer bookstore in the world. It prides itself on being an inclusive, safe space, and an alternative to the plentiful gay bars that fill the same area. Here was somewhere where you could congregate in a supportive environment without the space being dominated by alcohol consumption, as welcoming on a Tuesday afternoon as on a Saturday night. It wasn't hard to find, even amongst all the other Pride flags. Its large window showed the place already half full of excited people, most of whom were busy with brunch rather than browsing books. As I was alone, I was seated at the bar, and even my coffee arrived in a cocktail glass. A substantial brunch soon followed that I enthusiastically washed down with mimosas. Alcohol may have been optional, but it was an option I was happy to take!

As could be expected, it was a diverse audience. The host singled me out as the sole Brit in the building, but I was not the only person who'd never been to a drag show before. I met a lovely woman named Katie from the Maritimes, who was chaperoning a fourteen-year-old aspiring drag artist. She invited me to join them at their table so I'd get a better view. When the show started, a Lebanese drag queen (with a full beard) lip-synced songs in Arabic to raise money for Palestine, then managed to do the splits on the bookstore counter in thigh high heeled boots. We all threw our five dollar bills at her enthusiastically as tips. It was raucous, ridiculous, and absolutely the best thing that I could have spent Sunday morning doing. It was completely unlike anything that ever happens in Regina.

With the noise and mimosas and the party atmosphere of the drag show, it was easy to forget that this was a bookstore first and foremost. Books – mainly modern, queer nonfiction – lined the walls on all sides. Katie and I made some time to browse before she left. She asked me if I recommended anywhere else they should visit, as they knew Toronto even less well than I did. I suggested Little Ghosts horror bookstore, and the teenager's face lit up at the idea.

This gave me a good excuse to talk to the lone bookseller about Glad Day itself. I had heard a little of their troubles before visiting. This was a bookstore where community support had been absolutely crucial to its survival. In the spring of 2024, after fifty-five years in business, Glad Day Books was facing eviction from its Church Street home. Their story sounded similar to mine: years of debts racking up, compounded by the pandemic lockdowns. This being Toronto, however, my substantial rent payment in Regina pales in comparison to the overheads that Glad Day were facing. So, they had taken the only option available to them: asking their community for help.

It worked.

True to form, it worked fabulously. The owner reported receiving over a thousand donations in the first 24 hours and raising $85,000 within the first few days alone. It was enough to secure their lease and carry on at least for the foreseeable future. This was a bookstore that was getting it right. Glad Day know who their customers are and are deeply entwined with the local neighbourhood. Their books, their events and their general appeal meant that even in a city the size of Toronto, it's possible to create a sense of belonging in a close-knit community, and that community will value its bookstore and support it through the tough times.

I am fairly certain that Regina will never get its own entirely-queer bookstore with drag queens hosting brunches. In terms of progressiveness and diversity, we've a long way to go. But the sense of community that Glad Day Books inspired is something I know can be achieved in Saskatchewan. I do enjoy feeling anonymous sometimes as a change of pace from the claustrophobia of a small town. But anonymous does not have to mean 'estranged.' I truly appreciate the communities that my bookstore caters to and is a part of. Small businesses rely on local support, and Glad Day Books provides an inspirational example of how important that community support can be in times of trouble.

Books bought: 1
Copies of *Stroll* found: 0
Coffees consumed: 1 and several mimosas

A Book Token, Possibly Cursed by a Monkey

In 1906, English author W.W. Jacobs published a short story titled 'The Monkey's Paw.' In it, the White family acquire a talisman, a severed monkey's paw, that has the power to grant them three wishes. The family are strongly advised not to use it. But of course they do, because what could be the harm of getting everything you ever wanted? The short story is a horror and the family are forced to suffer the consequences in an extreme version of the adage, 'be careful what you wish for.'[7]

I mention this because there is a bookstore in Toronto called The Monkey's Paw and it was, in fact, everything I could wish for in one small storefront.

Monkey's Paw Books was established in 2006, exactly one hundred years after *The Monkey's Paw* story was published. The store aimed to stock used, rare, and antiquarian books on 'obsolete opinions and technologies,' from the 'age of print' – that is, the 20th century. That sounded a little disheartening at first, as it read as though print was now an obsolete medium. The store was working hard to dispel that rhetoric. Monkey's Paw also promised books as artefacts and 'earnest works on highly specific topics.' I hoped that could include a copy of *Stroll*, but then I read that they won't stock anything published after 1980. When they said 'vintage,' they really meant it.

---

[7] If this sounds like a familiar tale, it might be because *The Simpsons* borrowed it for a Treehouse of Horror episode in 1991. It also turned up in *The X Files* and *The Twilight Zone*. The 1990s were a great time for cursed tokens and unintended consequences.

Nevertheless, I found countless treasures within. The store appeared quite sparsely stocked at first, but as every single book had been selected and curated by the very passionate owners, it made for a fascinating collection. I now understood what was meant by 'books as artefacts.' Monkey's Paw was less of a bookstore in the conventional sense and more of a museum or a bibliophile's dream exhibition gallery. The store owner also trades with collectors and actively encourages people to bring in their most obscure books. This seemed to demonstrate a profound confidence; usually most used bookstores like the ones I had just visited have to vet the books to see if what is being donated or sold to the store is actually commercially viable. The only things that places like Seekers or Balfour Books would take were titles that the store owners thought would appeal to other people and have some resale value. Here in Monkey's Paw, the opposite seemed to be true; the more niche the appeal or the more unusual the title, the more the store was interested in it.

The bookstore contained everything I didn't know I needed: an entire book of 1940s font designs, for instance, and one on *Bread Sculpture - The Edible Art*. My own book collection now seemed so mainstream and inadequate in comparison. I very nearly bought a Penguin Paperback classic edition of *The Threepenny Novel* by Bertolt Brecht – mainly because 'Threepenny' will obviously be the name of my future third branch of The Penny University Bookstore. Unfortunately, the book cost quite a lot more than three pennies.

Prices aside, I was utterly enthralled by Monkey's Paw. Here was somewhere that was truly embracing their passions and owning their relative weirdness and, crucially, *making money from it*. I have long been scared that most of my entrepreneurial ideas are too outlandish to have sufficient appeal to the wider community, or to fulfil the fairly crucial business aim of turning a profit. Yet here was proof that you could be blatantly 'old and unusual,' indulge every eccentricity, stock books like the five-volume *Guide to the History of The Elevator*[8] and still, somehow, pay the rent. I was incredulous, but also awed.

The girl behind the counter was quite Goth, which suited her surroundings perfectly. She said her customers ranged from the earnest folks seeking exceedingly specific editions (the hardcore book collectors), and then the 'tourists' who came in to see The Bibliomat. I found myself more in the latter category than the former. I had read about this machine before finding The Monkey's Paw, and even saw it in action on Instagram. It does warrant the touristy hype around it.

---

[8] A book that entertains on many levels.

The Bibliomat is a book vending machine. Not just any vending machine either; the whole sky blue-coloured box is opaque, with the token slot on the side and a small open slot at the bottom. Around eye-height, it says simply "Bibliomat." Otherwise, there are no instructions and no clues as to what will be dispensed from its slot. The Bibliomat is the world's first *randomised* book vending machine. The machine alone knew what book it would bestow upon you. I thought of the monkey's paw plot… what horrendous consequences would befall me if I used this magical machine?

I decided to take my chances. I paid the Goth girl $5, which she exchanged for a small, ominous-looking token. Pushing the token into the Bibliomat machine gave a very satisfying THUNK and then a book landed in the slot near my ankles. It was wrapped in a strip of white paper and fastened with a sticker with Monkey Paw's star shaped logo and the words "Old & Unusual" around the edge. This relatable slogan meant it was definitely the one for me. I received a 106-year-old hardcover book of exciting war stories featuring a brigade of soldiers from New Zealand. Apparently, according to the inside cover flaps, "no boy alive will be able to peruse its pages without a quickening of his pulses." I brought it home to test its effects on Milo. So far, no heart palpitations, although he told me he did enjoy the *smell* of the book.

As wonderful as it was to see the bookstore, there was also something unsettling about the place. As I left the store, the thought did occur to me that the space would instantly fold in on itself and vanish with a pop as soon as I stepped foot outside. Or if I dared look back at it from across the street, I would be forever damned. "Don't turn around, don't turn around" I told myself furtively as I walked. Maybe Monkey's Paw exists in an alternate dimension, and if I ever tried to visit again, I will find no trace of it – the website will be gone, Instagram will be scrubbed clean of any references to the Bibliomat, and the Goth girl will return to work at Type Books and will not know what I am talking about if I ask about her stint at the infamous Monkey's Paw…

I am recording these words, my memories of this place, so that in the event of my demise, readers shall know the Monkey's Paw token was indeed cursed, and be warned…

Books bought: 1
Copies of *Stroll* found: 0
Coffees consumed: 0

Famous Last Words

The Toronto International Festival of Authors (TIFA) teaches me a great deal every year. There is always something new to discover, so many different writing styles and genres to learn about, and a huge range of authors participating. The events I attended covered everything from the cultural significance of dumplings, and why the Moomins are timeless, to writing war correspondence and retelling Greek myths by setting them in the Caribbean. Most importantly, it taught me that authors come in many forms.

The first time I attended TIFA was in 2022, at which time I'd had two books traditionally published and was working on my third. Even still, I did not feel like an 'author.' I rationalised this feeling because I don't write fiction, and I don't make a living from my writing. I am a book*seller*: I just sell the work of authors… But TIFA made me appreciate that I, too, am an author. I do *write* books as well as sell them! That was a very welcome discovery. I decided to treat myself to cocktails to celebrate this revelation. What better place to sip tiny, expensive drinks than a bar lined with bookshelves, featuring cocktails inspired by the great works of literature? Such a bar does exist in Toronto, and it is called 'Famous Last Words.'

Unfortunately, Famous Last Words was a long way out from the Harbourfront where the TIFA events took place. I had prepaid for the Toronto bike share scheme though, and at that point, it was not raining. On the map, it looked like a fairly easy bike ride west along the lake's edge via the Martin Goodman trail, and then up through High Park until I reached the Junction neighbourhood. About forty minutes, I thought. Famous Last Words indeed.

I unhooked a now-familiar green bike from the rack of them on Queen's Quay, set up the navigation app on my phone, balanced it precariously on the handlebars, and set out. At first, I was grateful for the abundance of public space and the bike paths that wove their way around the top of Lake Ontario. They are well-maintained, wide, and in the early evening, surprisingly empty. Most importantly, they kept me out of the rush hour traffic that clogged the downtown core. However, the disadvantage of sticking to these paths was that they significantly increased the distance.

The most direct route to the Junction area is to find Dundas Street and follow it north-west. Dundas is one of the few streets in Toronto that doesn't follow the grid system. Instead, it meanders gently from southeast to northwest, and it has corners in it! As tempting as this was, I decided it unwise to cycle on a major thoroughfare just as the whole city was leaving work in their cars, especially when car-free paths were an option. This logic suited me well until the paths gave way to sidewalks, and I lost sight of the lake for orientation.

At the western end of the trail, I found myself in the Canadian National Exhibition grounds. I have never been to CNE, but the much-smaller Saskatchewan equivalent, called 'Queen City Ex' has formed an expensive staple in my kids' summer holidays for many years already. The Exhibition had long gone by late September, and in the dim of the evening, the empty CNE grounds looked forlorn and sad. It was ever so slightly eerie, too. There could easily be a killer clown hiding around any corner. I decided it would make an excellent set for yet another post-apocalyptic disaster movie. I pedalled around in circles for a while, out of curiosity more than orienteering, and I didn't see another living soul.

Moving swiftly on, I caught sight of the lake again and continued skirting the edge until my phone confidently told me to cross under the Gardiner Expressway. It was here that things started to go very wrong.

From a cyclist's point of view, there is nothing to love about the Gardiner Expressway except the fact that cycling on it is forbidden. It is a psychological – and sometimes physical – barrier separating the inviting public space of the lakeside with the rest of the city. This means that crossing it, usually underneath it via a long dark underpass, is a necessary evil. Suddenly, there were no more comforting bike lanes. Instead, beneath the incessant torrent of cars on the expressway, were four dark, narrow lanes of traffic running under both the expressway and the Queensway bypass. The raised sidewalk was inexplicably closed by some construction work and it was too late to cross and use the one on the left. I had no lights on my rental bike and the sun was setting fast. I also realised that I was wearing my black rain jacket too, rendering me nearly invisible in the gloom. This was going to be neither safe nor fun. I reluctantly wove into the cars and pedalled as fast as the heavy bike's third gear would allow me.

I made it through the underpass without anything hitting me, but I was still on a major road without a helmet nor anything to make me more visible. It was rapidly getting dark. Worse, using the navigation tracking on my phone with the volume on maximum was killing the battery. I bumped up onto the sidewalk and studied the little map carefully. I was on Parkside Drive that runs north on the edge of High Park. But in the park itself were several clearly marked trails. Those would be much better to ride on, I thought. I'd be fine in the park, and as long as I headed north-ish, I'd be more or less parallel with the road anyway. With that fairly sensible decision I decided to save my phone battery for the return journey and switched it off.

Saying the park was dark was an understatement. I had underestimated the number of trees and overestimated the amount of streetlights. By this time, it was dusk and with a good dose of pathetic fallacy, it started to rain again as well. The path I'd chosen that seemed to be heading northwest suddenly swung south again with little warning and no alternative route in sight. I kept going, thinking it was just full of twists and turns as opposed to the strict grid of the roads. Soon, there were more lights up ahead. That could only be a good thing, I reasoned.

By the time I reached the source of the lights, I was cold, wet, out of patience, and still nowhere near where I wanted to be. This whole trip had been a stupid idea! My mood did not improve when I saw that the source of the lights was… High Park Zoo. I definitely did not need to be near the zoo. I had gone seriously off course, somewhere, and I didn't even know where. Frustrated, I pulled the phone out again, hoping that I had enough battery life left for the location tracker to find me. The trees and the rainclouds and the low battery did not help, but eventually the stoic Google voice told me to "head north for 400 metres." But the only 'north' I could go was straight through the closed zoo!

That was the final straw, and I kicked my poor bike. I knew that retracing my steps would lead me back to the road, which would now be even darker and more dangerous on two wheels. Or I could do as Google seemed to suggest and leave the paved path and wiggle randomly through trees around the edge of the zoo. Or, and this option seemed the 'least worst,' I could dump the bike at the handily placed rental bike rack, walk back to the main road, and hope that there was a bus route on it.

By the time I got back to the road, I was beginning to panic. I had now lost my sense of direction entirely, as walking never feels as direct for me as cycling does. I no longer cared if I got to the bar, but I also didn't know how to get back to the Airbnb where I was staying. All I knew was that I needed to get somewhere, and that somewhere was not High Park.

Yet again, I was saved by the Toronto Transport Commission. Relief flooded in as I exited the park and saw a bus stop right in front of me. Better yet, there was a man standing in it, implying that a bus was not far away. I crossed the road and stood next to him, dripping gently. Soon enough, a sleek red bus appeared and we both clambered aboard. I waved my Presto card limply at the sensor, not knowing if I actually had any money left on the card. I hadn't even seen where the bus was headed.

I watched out the window, frantically trying to recognise any feature of the dark surroundings to regain my bearings. The stops noted on the bus's screen were meaningless to me. It took an agonisingly long time, but eventually the scrolling red letters on the bus screen said Dundas Street West. Now I knew where I was! I got off the bus gratefully and changed onto the streetcar. The rails in the road led reassuringly in one direction only. There could be no more getting lost. A few minutes later, I could see Famous Last Words! Its teal-blue sign lit up like a beacon. "Welcome weary traveller," it seemed to say.

Famous Last Words was everything I needed it to be at that point: safe, warm, welcoming, and filled with strong alcohol. I felt a little underdressed as I entered, still in my rain jacket and leggings. This was definitely a classy establishment. However, the sensation soon faded; I had made it! It had taken me more than twice as long as I'd planned, I was tired and cold, I hadn't eaten anything, and I felt a little remorseful about taking my frustration out on the bike. But I was triumphant. I cast around looking at all the classic books on the shelves in the bar. After that journey, I felt like Odysseus, Phileas Fogg, 'Pi' Patel and maybe even Frodo Baggins all rolled into one. *What would these fictional voyagers be drinking?* I wondered.

The bar was long and narrow, lined on two sides by floor-to-ceiling bookshelves. The bar counter was mosaicked with Scrabble tiles. It faced a fireplace framed with a mantel on which sat beautifully dribbly candles poked into whiskey bottles. The whiskey in question was called 'Writers' Tears.' I sat down in a vintage winged armchair in front of the fire and immediately regretted this – the chair was soft enough that I didn't think I'd be able to get out of it again. There was a low coffee table in front of me, glass topped with yellowing book pages underneath. To my relief, a server came over, negating the need for me to move. "Are you here for the book group?" she asked. I shook my head, but felt instantly inspired. A cocktail-fueled book group! That would be fun. Not for the first time, I contemplated getting an alcohol licence for my own bookstore.

The Famous Last Words cocktail menu is extensive and impressive. I would have loved to have tried the Writers' Tears whiskey combinations, but whiskey is the one evil spirit that I cannot stomach. I am a very British gin drinker, or, if my budget allows, a rum guzzler. The best options for my tastes on the menu were 'The Mystery at Lilac Inn' (inspired by the Nancy Drew mystery by Carolyn Keene). It promised 'purple gin,' and it did not disappoint. I didn't think I'd ever encountered purple spirits before. Feeling creative, I began writing my journal by candlelight in scratchy fountain pen as I drank. Playing the part of 'tortured writer' now came easily to me as the rain poured down outside. As the madness of the day settled into my brain, I chose the 'Don Quixote' cocktail next. It involved Mezcal… that's all I remember. My journal becomes illegible at this point.

I am not sure if the books at Famous Last Words were actually for sale or merely decoration, but the resident book group was noisy and animated. Buoyed on by my newly-realised status as Proper Author and with confidence boosted by the alcohol, I slid a copy of my own book into the shelves above the fireplace. The best authors all have their vices, and only a real author would carry around copies of their own book in the rain and on a bike for use in these opportune moments as they prop up a bar. I vowed then that one day I should turn my adventures into another book.

"Always do sober what you said you'd do drunk. That will teach you to keep your mouth shut." - Ernest Hemingway.

Dear reader, I do apologise.

Books bought: 0.
Copies of *Stroll* found: 0
Coffees bought: 0. Several cocktails, though.

Part 4: East

Mother Bird

For the first time on this trip, I ventured slightly east of Spadina Avenue. Spadina is my spine in Toronto. Its general walkability, wide sidewalks and racks of shared bikes, its colourfulness and its proximity to cheap lodgings and interesting eats, makes me naturally gravitate towards it. If you travel far enough north on Spadina, you end up at a castle - Casa Loma - that looks out over the city. This was a very welcome discovery for me, and soon Spadina became my main north-south passage.

A few blocks east of Spadina, where the rain painted the streets in slick, glistening hues, lay the University of Toronto Bookstore near St. George Street. A behemoth of academia, its façade loomed over the sidewalks and cycle paths. The older style of architecture with stone pillars and 'frilly bits at the top' create a monolithic presence amidst the urban sprawl of Starbucks branches and half-million-dollar condos that surround it. There was a little paved courtyard in front of it, hedged on two sides with a stone bench in between. I sat on the bench and immediately regretted it as I felt the dampness seep in. The place would probably be attractive if it wasn't January, but this was the time of year when the cold permeated my bones. The rain fell with a relentless determination, a bleak backdrop that reminded me of my own university days in the English rain. Academia will always be somewhat cold, wet, miserable, and grey.

A word of explanation is needed here.

The University of Toronto Press (UTP) is the 'Mother Bird' to many Canadian independent bookstores. Not only does the university press publish a considerable number of titles of its own, but the company distributes books for many other smaller publishers as well. Book distribution is an impenetrably complex industry, with small presses feeding books to larger ones who in turn feed them to even bigger, but more hidden distributors who hoard and lovingly catalogue all those books. Then they disperse them once again to our tiny bookstores across the country. We are fledgling chicks, squawking around blindly with our mouths open, waiting for Mother to feed us. The University of Toronto Press is one such Mother Bird, and she is mighty.

Much like Penguin Random House, the UTP Mother is not somewhere where one can just walk into uninvited. Instead, I have an intensely needy, one-sided relationship with a person named Shammy who is my sales rep at UTP. I have never met them, or even spoken to them, but they fulfil most of my bookish desires – eventually. I do know my place in the pecking order of the bookstore world. It is fairly near the bottom, since I do not have the buying power of multi-branch chain stores. As such, Shammy does respond to my demands, but only after making me wait and beg and plead and pay upfront. I debated whether to contact them and ask to visit, but thought better of it. Some relationships are best left long distance.

Instead, I focused on the main UTP Bookstore, open to students and the public alike. I stepped inside, the warmth of the store a stark contrast to the chill outside. My glasses steamed up instantaneously, and as I wiped them clean, I was momentarily stunned. For a second, I thought that I was in the wrong building again. There were no books to be seen! Instead, I was greeted by rack upon rack of UofT branded clothing – hoodies, t-shirts, baseball caps, even teddy bears wearing mini UofT sweaters. If you wanted it, this store had it with a University logo slapped across it. Aside from the clothing, there were also branded notebooks and pens, and then earphone holders, USB cable tidies, desk lamps, laptop sleeves and more, all emblazoned with the now familiar blue and white insignia. But no books.

I approached the cash desk. Extremely self-conscious at my own ridiculousness, I asked the cashier where the books were. The cashier was a stern-looking woman with a very sensible ponytail. She raised one eyebrow at me, incredulously, and gestured upstairs. Of course a bookstore wouldn't have books displayed in the entrance! No, in this temple to the pursuit of higher learning, one must look beyond the surface, face ridicule, and seek out the treasure for oneself.

Sure enough, on the second floor, the aisles stretched out before me, lined with towering shelves of knowledge. The new semester had only just begun when I visited, so the store was unusually busy with students panic-buying textbooks and supplies for their new modules. Those were the $200 textbooks that it is mandatory to purchase for your already expensive course. The costs are then compounded by the built-in obsolescence: the books are updated every year rendering older editions defunct. I still have my anthropology textbooks from my undergraduate degree at home. They are gathering dust, unopened in perhaps twenty years. I know I can never part with them, because the painful memory of their price tags still haunts me to this day.

As I made my way through the maze of books, I couldn't shake the feeling of being watched. I glanced around and my eyes finally settled on him – a man of formidable presence in a dark blue shirt and neat facial hair, standing ominously in the corner. He was not moving and did not make eye contact when I looked across at him, but his gaze was piercing, like he could see right through me. Between him and the unsmiling cashier, I feel more than a little intimidated. I imagine I cut an unlikely figure in a place like this: damp and bedraggled and rather lost. I was neither a tourist buying the branded teddy bears, nor a conscientious student spending their loan. Given the costs of those precious tomes before me, I can forgive the staff for being suspicious. Nevertheless, this must have been the first bookstore I've ever visited that has its own security guard.

Finally, I discovered the sections I'd been looking for: the 'trade' books, as opposed to hardcore academia. I even spotted a few titles from the University of Regina Press, their bright orange logo jumping out at me happily from the shelves. I picked up an introductory guide to Psychology for Milo. It was unlikely that he would want undergraduate level reading material in Grade 8, but he has already expressed an interest in attending UofT. I want to encourage these ambitions.

As I made my way through the Humanities, I felt certain I must, at last, be in luck. Surely, they must have a copy of *Stroll* in here? Shawn Micallef teaches a course called 'Engaging Toronto' at the university, although I can't remember if UTP distributes his books. I head straight for the social geography section and eagerly scan down to the 'M' shelf.

Nothing. The shelf is not just missing *Stroll,* but there are no Micallefs at all. Thwarted again.

To make myself feel better, I purchased a book that seemed to leap out at me. It is a graphic novel, except it isn't a novel. *Fast Forward* is a collection of essays about imagined, plausible urban futures presented in comic form, and it was unlike anything I've seen in a university bookstore before. Even better, it was in the Bargain section for $6. I pounced on it. The stern cashier seemed relieved that I was buying something, finally.

As I left the store, the rain intensified, the sky a dismal grey above me. I pulled my heavy winter coat tighter around me and started out towards a transit stop. I may not have seen The Mother Bird in her full glory, and I may not have found *Stroll*, but I had found some interesting titles. My newly acquired books felt gloriously solid and reassuring in my bag. Onwards!

Books bought: 2
Copies of *Stroll* found: 0
Coffees consumed: 0

A Stroll Along the Danforth

In the heat of mid-July during my fourth and more impromptu trip to Toronto, I decided it was a good idea to cycle along Danforth Avenue from Kensington Market. The six kilometre eastbound trip would take me past at least four bookstores that I hadn't properly visited on previous excursions. My mental map of Toronto was improving too, and I'd just learned that Bloor Street wriggles a little over the river, and then turns into 'the Danforth.' (I do not know why Danforth gets its own definite article, but colloquially it does, a little like 'the Yukon'). I had previously stayed in Hostel #1 at the eastern end of Danforth Avenue and I really could have done with figuring out its proximity to Bloor Street on that occasion. Instead, I spent that trip cycling due south to get to the Harbourfront and on one notable occasion, ending up at the beach unexpectedly. This was disconcerting but not unpleasant, but I now knew there were far easier ways to get to the downtown core.

This time, however, the Danforth ride was extremely hot and sticky as the weather was topping 30 degrees, but it was an easy one. The only slightly unnerving part was crossing the Prince Edward Viaduct where the cycle lane was very obviously added as an afterthought. It wasn't the traffic that was frightening – at least, no more frightening than usual – but it was the sheer height of the bridge and the drop down to the receded Don River below. I had not noticed pedaling uphill from the western side of the river, and the safety of the other side did not slope downwards either. This made the drop beneath the bridge feel unnatural, as if a chasm had just opened up in the middle of the city, rather than the city being built over top of the chasm.

I was on one of the Bike Share bikes, and the only problem I had with this route was having to cycle past the bookstore I was aiming for to find somewhere to dock the bike. Danforth is a strange mix of styles: the closer to the river you are, the more gentrified the street is. At the beginning of the avenue, there are bike racks and planters full of flowers, and a tiny pedestrianised area with trees and benches and an I Heart Toronto sculpture. The little street ends in The Big Carrot Community Market.

Heading east on Danforth out towards the hostel takes you through Greek Town; the businesses get older and soon every other building is some sort of restaurant (not just Greek, either. I had a delicious Ethiopian curry in that area, too. The server laughed at me for needing cutlery). The street names are labelled in Greek first, then English, and all the lamp posts and poles have the Greek flag on them. The hostel I stayed in is flanked by a Dim Sum House, a convenience store and cell phone repair shop, and the job centre (permanently closed, apparently). The next block east is dominated by the Madinah Masjid Mosque complete with towering minaret atop it. Take any road going south from there and you are met with a steep hill heading down through the largely residential Leslieville neighbourhood. Going down the hills on the bike was fun. Heading back up them was not.

Danforth Avenue is extremely long, and if you follow the road entirely you will end up in Scarborough. Alternatively, veering off the avenue at the last minute lands you on a very pretty, quiet beach with a great many new and expensive-looking properties surrounding it. I did allow myself an afternoon at the beach, but most of the time I didn't stray further east than the hostel and Donlands metro station. The bookstores I was interested in are all west of the hostel.

On my first trip, I came across Circus Books and Music, a used bookstore with CDs and vinyl as well. It took me a while to get in: the shop opens seven days a week, but only from 11am. Having gone out unusually early for me (one of my hostel dorm mates had set his alarm for 5am), I hung around forlornly outside waiting for the place to open. This did give me the opportunity to browse their exceptionally well-curated window display. For a used bookstore, their range was vast and I spotted a great many interesting titles that I'd never heard of. There were even books in other languages, which is a rare sight in used stores. It was clear that the stock pickers were collecting books from a diverse range of suppliers.

I went back later in the afternoon and found the place full of people. Everyone seemed to know each other and there was an animated discussion happening about the merits of a particular jazz album on vinyl that someone had unearthed in the back of the store. Circus Books is obviously a community staple. It was also the first Toronto bookstore I'd come across where other customers seemed to want to chat to me. I was immediately distracted by this and could not choose a book to buy as a result; all the customers had recommendations for me! Paralysed by indecision, I let a woman tell me about a middle-grade chapter book that her children had loved about talking rabbits. So I bought it, and as the lady predicted, my daughter enjoyed it very much.

***

I knew there were a few bookstores to visit at the opposite (western) end of the Danforth, but I discovered one called Scribe that I hadn't noticed when I was planning my route. Scribe Books is an elegant little store squashed in on the south side of Danforth Avenue, and its stock is also beautiful. I confess, I was so hot after my bike ride that I did not want to spend much time in a store that just had a large fan to relieve the oppressive July heat, but I thought I should venture in anyway. I was glad I did. Scribe specialises in antiquarian books, collectors editions, and art prints. The Folio Society editions (exceptionally pretty hardcover editions of classic literature) contrasted nicely with a display of vintage paperbacks with the 1970s B-movie art on the covers.

Scribe also has a large range of books with Victorian bindings – the sort that look like if you pulled the right one out of the shelf, a secret door would open, allowing you into a vault full of gold. No such vault appeared for me, but I did notice a closed off area at the back where the rarest of books were kept and trades were made with serious book collectors. I realised this was not my world. I do collect books, but I care more about their content rather than their year of publication or their format. I will admit to being sorely tempted by the Folio Society books, but I would have to acquire dozens of them to create the 'eccentric aristocrat's library' effect that they inspire. Unfortunately, neither my budget nor my backpack allowed for that. I spotted a place opposite that promised me an iced latte, so I took my leave from Scribe before I overheated.

***

Coffee in hand, I found myself back at Carrot Common, the newish and attractive little pedestrianised side street. It sadly lacked giant carrots, as far I could tell anyway, but it did have a branch of Book City. Book City is another store that sells both new and bargain books. It was spacious, cheerfully yellow on the outside, and deliciously air conditioned on the inside. The bookseller behind the counter was busy collecting online orders and labelling them for pick up, constantly moving from a computer screen to the receipt printer to a stack of books and back again. I recognised the task well from my own store and did not envy her. She took the time to tell me more about Book City though, describing the business as 'fiercely independent' and wishing me well both for my own indie store and for my Toronto bookstore quest. Book City has four branches around the city, including another in The Beaches area that she recommended I try as I was 'on vacation.' Whereas I would probably have enjoyed a beach-side bookstore, the thought of cycling out there and then all the way back to Kensington Market again in that heat rapidly put me off the idea.

Book City had a great selection of nonfiction, and I was hopeful that there might at last be a copy of Micallef's *Stroll*. But sadly, I did not see it. Instead, I found a new anthology of 'women writing about walking.' Almost, almost, psychogeography! This was an excellent substitute and I felt triumphant, despite the book being heavy and unfortunately not in the bargain section.

I unlocked another Bike Share bike and made sure to strap my purchases onto the handlebar rack securely. I had visions of them slipping and plummeting off the viaduct on the way back, but my return journey was uneventful. I reached the other hostel tired and hot but very happy. Danforth Avenue held considerable surprises – not just the unexpected discovery of Scribe and the book on walking, but the sheer variety of places, styles, and people found on one long and vibrant street. The Danforth felt a little like Kensington Market, but without the tourists. I think it could be one of my favourite parts of Toronto.

Books bought: 2
Copies of *Stroll* found: 0
Coffees consumed: one hot, one iced.

Re:Reading

Bookstore owners are, at risk of massive generalisation, a fairly odd bunch. I include myself in this statement. On top of the general precariousness of entrepreneurship, it does seem to take a special kind of person to dedicate their existence to hunting out, curating, and displaying so many tomes, only to sell them again and having to restart the process. In his lengthy book on the subject, (that I picked up at a BMV branch) Nicholas Basbanes calls bibliomania 'the gentle madness.' The more bookstores I visit, the more I see how prevalent this madness may be.

Given that some level of eccentricity appears to be a prerequisite, it is inevitable that the other passions of the owner gradually leak into the bookstore as well. This was evident in some of the stores in Toronto that I had already visited: the Lego in Doug Miller Books, for instance, and the jazz records in Circus Books and Music. My own Penny University Bookstore has a coffee bar in it, and coffee paraphernalia, and an entire shelf dedicated to books about coffee, all a hangover from my previous ventures in what now feels like another life.

This display of 'outside interests' was no more apparent than in Re:Reading, the fourth bookstore I visited on Danforth Avenue. Re:Reading is a red-painted used bookstore, with a little robot dog as their logo. The dog alone should have been a clue as to the shop's contents, reminiscent as it was of K9 from Doctor Who, but it turned out that the owner was not just a Whovian. Above the counter was a vast collection of Star Trek character bobbleheads, all artfully displayed. A model of the Starship Enterprise hung overhead. On the opposite wall to the counter was what appeared to be a shrine to all things Trek: a velvet display stand of Starfleet Academy pins, posters, signed photos of cast members, and the jewel of the collection: a Starfleet uniform with the insignia replaced by the bookstore's dog logo. I knew that

there are novelisations of the Star Trek series and no doubt a huge number of fan fiction volumes too, but the collection in Re:Reading was unexpectedly impressive.

Equally impressive was the store's commitment to the book community and to supporting local. Under the glass countertop, I spotted two hand drawn maps[9] showing the locations

---

[9] These were the same maps I'd come across at Another Story Bookstore in Roncesvalle, but chronologically speaking, I discovered them first in Re:Reading. Long after I returned from Toronto and began processing these adventures, I learned that the maps were originally drawn by the owner of Little Ghosts. This fact makes me profoundly happy.

of other indie bookstores! It was delightfully fitting that I should find a treasure map to aid me on my epic quest in a store full of tales of fantastical voyages and exploration. The two maps had been created to split Toronto into east and west, much like I was semi-consciously doing myself. I was relieved to find I had already come across all the indie stores on the west map, but there were at least three on the east map that I hadn't heard of, yet. I asked the bookseller about the maps, and she explained that they had been made for Independent Bookstore Day that year (Canadian Independent Bookstore Day is usually the last weekend of April, so when I found them, the maps were fairly new). She did not know who drew them unfortunately, but she allowed me to take photos of them to guide me on my mission. The bookish community in Regina is close knit, mainly because Regina is so small. It was quite heartwarming to see that so many of the different store owners seemed to know each other and support each other across a city as big as Toronto.

The vast majority of used bookstores are 'general interest' as it is much harder to amass enough stock if you're only finding used books in a specific genre. Re:Reading did stock many different genres and topics and even had a shelf of staff picks, (and, adorably, "My Mom's Recommendations"). But the largest portion of the store was devoted to science fiction. In the main area of the store, there were Sci-Fi and Fantasy hardcovers, and then another section devoted to Speculative Fiction. At the back of the store and above my head, I saw a neon-coloured unicorn that informed me that the space I was about to enter was called Quantum Unicorn.

Through a doorway, I could see Doctor Who's Tardis against one wall. (The Tardis is the Doctor's time travelling spaceship and defies the normal laws of physics by being bigger on the inside. This bookstore certainly created the same illusion.) The lampshades inside Quantum Unicorn were in the form of the Death Star from Star Wars. Bruce Willis as John McClane (from the Die Hard movie) appeared to be crawling out of the air ducts. A black bookshelf on the far wall opened out to reveal Han Solo's carbonised form, and light sabres hung above it, still glowing. The centrepiece, though, was a large map of the Earth and the immediate solar system around it. Arrows surrounded our planet, directing you to such fantastic places as Gallifrey (from Doctor Who) and Vulcan (Star Trek), and then more literary worlds: Hogwarts, Narnia, Neverland, Pratchett's Discworld, Panem (Hunger Games), and Westeros (Game of Thrones). Underneath, books were crammed into every available space between the paraphernalia, from aging paperbacks to entire series in matching hardcovers. Every conceivable fandom was represented. The owners had created their very own fan convention hall in the back of their small shop, and it was a wonder to behold.

I spent considerable time in the stuffy, cramped space, thoroughly enjoying trying to identify the stranger artefacts in there. My knowledge of more obscure sci-fi turned out to be woefully inadequate for this store. My eye was caught by a painted mirror at chest height, with a small sign next to it saying:

"Align Head Here and Take Photo."

I obeyed, and found that in my picture, my face had deformed and contorted and I was sporting a metal plate over one eye. My neck and shoulders were now those of a steel-framed cyborg, with green lights flashing all over. I had been assimilated to the Borg. Resistance was futile.

Now more convinced than ever that I would never be able to leave this bookstore of my own accord, I desperately tried to remember which Stephen Baxter books I already owned and whether or not my husband would ever read the full collection of James Corey's *The Expanse* series if I got him the matching set. A purchase felt necessary: I think Re:Reading could justify charging an entrance fee and calling the Quantum Unicorn space a Sci-Fi museum!

Then, with reluctance, I remembered I was cycling and supposedly travelling light. I would just have to content myself with the sweet knowledge that such collections exist in the world, and that booksellers can succeed when they allow themselves to put their other passions on display as well. We booksellers may be an eccentric group, but we embrace our geekishness cheerfully.

Books bought: 0 (but not for lack of desire)
Copies of *Stroll* found: 0
Coffees consumed: 0

There's Something About McNally

'McNally' is a good name for booksellers. In the prairies, there are two branches of McNally Robinson Booksellers, one in Winnipeg and one in Saskatoon. In Manhattan, there is an indie bookstore called McNally Jackson, owned by the daughter of the McNally couple who founded the Canadian version. In Toronto, there is Ben McNally Books. As far as I can work out, Ben is not related to the other bookselling dynasty. He has 'semi-retired' though, and now his children are running the Toronto store instead. Bookselling appears to be a hereditary condition.

As I set out for Toronto for the second time, I began reading up on the bookstores. There are several 'city-guide' style blogs in Toronto and in them I found a few listing the Top Ten Bookstores in Toronto and similar listicles. Several of them named Ben McNally Books as 'the most beautiful bookstore' in the city, and 'a hidden gem.' The store has been around for nearly two decades and is definitely well known with an intensely loyal following. Located on the western end of Queen Street East, with a handy number of bike share docks nearby, I was looking forward to visiting.

I must admit, I was a bit underwhelmed when I found the store. I cycled past it more than once because it did not catch my eye at all as I passed. I eventually docked my bike nearby where I thought the store must be and started walking instead, hoping that more would be visible on foot. At the time of my visit, most of that block of Queen Street was under construction and the bookstore was fairly easy to miss under a mound of scaffolding. I found it eventually but with a very temporary-looking canvas banner pinned up outside it. To its right was a vape shop, and the vape shop had better signage. Definitely a rarity. The bookstore's canvas banner had the slogan 'Read the fine print' underneath the store name, which I do consider a work of genius.

Inside, it looked…okay. Ben McNally's is not a large store, but the unit is deep and the place seemed to stretch back a long way from its meagre entrance. I ventured in, looking for *Stroll*, but also for a specific book for my daughter. As a general interest store, I hoped Ben McNally might just have both.

The dark wood bookshelves are built into the walls at Ben McNally's and round tables piled high dot the remaining floor space. There were no free-standing shelves and the space looked cosy and neat without being cluttered. Of course, I had to be That Person who pulled a book out from the end of a lower shelf and knocked the entire shelf of books sideways in doing so, but the booksellers were very polite about it.

At the 2022 Toronto International Festival of Authors, author Ben Clayton had been a guest speaker at the kids events. Clayton writes and illustrates the *Narwhal and Jelly* graphic novels, (amongst other books). My daughter Theia loves *Narwhal and Jelly* and was bitterly disappointed both that she couldn't come with me, and that I hadn't arrived in Toronto in time to attend the TIFA Kids Festival held the weekend before the main events. With this emotional imperative, I felt I had to find the appropriate Narwhal volume elsewhere.

At first inspection, I thought I would be in luck with both titles. Ben McNally's stock is small, but exceptionally well-curated. No copies of *Stroll*, however, although the bookseller there (not, I assume, Ben McNally himself although possibly his son) immediately offered to order it in for me. I admired the speed at which he offered, even though I couldn't accept. (I would not be in Toronto long enough to pick it up.) This, I knew, was a crucial part of independent bookstore business structure: there is no way for small stores like McNally's – and my own – to stock absolutely every book that anyone could ever want. The trick is to make ordering the books as smooth and as pleasant an experience as possible. Not only is the personalized order remembered by customers, it's also an excellent way for the booksellers to keep track of popular books and current trends. Special orders are something that larger multi-branch stores struggle with and where independents have the advantage.

Unfortunately, the *Narwhal and Jelly* title for Theia was also a 'special order' in Ben McNally's. They have a rather vintage children's section, with picture books that were old when I was a child – *Peepo* and *Each Peach Pear Plum* by Janet and Allan Ahlberg, the *Madeleine* series, and *Goodnight Moon*. I am exceedingly grateful for the fact that my children have long since grown out of the rhyming, repetitive traditions of bedtime stories, even if I do now have to read about Narwhals out loud at 9pm every night. Overall, I was a bit disappointed with McNally's. I had high hopes and expectations for the city's most beautiful bookstore and it was rather mediocre compared to the glowing reviews online.

As it turned out, I was too quick to judge. I needed to read the fine print, as their banner stated. I looked up the history of Ben McNally's as soon as I returned to my lodgings, and instantly forgave the temporary banner and nondescript decor.

Ben McNally's Bookstore has had to move locations three times in three years. They were originally located on Bay Street, right in the heart of Toronto's financial district and close to the huge Eaton's centre. This was the location that was voted 'most beautiful.' Their original store had high vaulted ceilings, similar built-in bookshelves, chandeliers, ornate pillars. and pendulum lights. The photos of it on their website are stunning! Unfortunately, they were refused a renewal on their lease after twelve years, (I do not know why) and were made 'homeless' just before the pandemic began.

Throughout the most difficult time many small businesses could imagine – the sporadic lockdowns, restrictions, and public health regulations of Covid-19 – the store had two different temporary homes before arriving at their Queen Street location in 2022. It is hard enough for a business to move once, especially after being so long established in the original location. But doing so three times in such a short period and all the while coping with the pandemic and *still* thriving, shows fierce determination, hope, and a level of bravery that I am awed by.

The fact that Ben McNally's is still operating at all, let alone running as a family business with a semi-retired owner is nothing short of remarkable. 'McNally' is a well-recognised name in the world of independent bookstores, and with good reason. Like the familiar titles in their children's section, they are nothing if not tenacious.

***

If I was asked to vote for 'the most beautiful' bookstore in Toronto, I would give my vote to another one in the east end: Queen Books. This store is another one that I cannot believe I missed originally. I made many trips along Queen Street East on my rental bikes, travelling between the hostel on the Danforth and the festival at Harbourfront, and yet every single time, I seemed to go right past it without noticing. This made my eventual visit even more satisfying.

I would describe Queen Books as 'a little bit bonkers' – which I mean in the most loving and sincere way. The outside of their small store is covered with kitsch plasterwork, depicting gaudy fake bookshelves all the way around the windows and front door. There are even alcoves along the side walls with more false book spines making a colourful, almost garish facade. Above your head as you enter are the heads and shoulders of a dozen little figures all holding up books. It is reminiscent of the saints in a Catholic church – all devoted to the sacred act of reading. There is absolutely no sleek, tidy minimalism here, and I was immediately drawn to it for that reason alone.

Like many other bookstores, it had a rustic chalkboard sign outside. As with McNally's bookstore further down the street, Queen Books had been mentioned in the 'best of Toronto' blogs. Their chalkboard read "We're number 20 of the 150 bookstores to visit before you die. Come on in!" The word 'die' had been obscured by a drawing of a bright yellow flower, in case you didn't need a casual *memento mori.*

Inside was equally colourful – another long, narrow unit with a raised area at the back, and all the new releases, staff choices, and best sellers stacked on round tables at the front. The cash desk held flyers for book groups and upcoming events. I was pleased to find that all the books indoors were real and not made of plaster, but I still checked, just in case.

For me, the highlight of the store was the waist-height cuddly giraffe in the children's section. Not only was it utterly unrelated to anything else – it wasn't a giraffe from a specific book, or the logo of a publisher, or part of an elaborate marketing campaign – it was simply a giraffe for the sake of being a giraffe in a bookstore. To my delight, it was also wearing a flat cap and nerdy plastic rimmed glasses.

Better still, I found not one, but all eight of the *Narwhal and Jelly* series, high on the shelf stocked with all manner of middle-grade graphic novels. I bought Theia an omnibus edition, feeling triumphant.

Unfortunately, Queen Books did not stock *Stroll*, although like their colleagues at McNally's they quickly offered to order it for me. Oh well, I thought, the giraffe more than makes up for the lack of *Stroll*. A few months later when he released the updated version of the book, Shawn Micallef held his book launch at Queen Books. I hope his event brought lots of customers to the store. Queen Books is beautiful because it is bold, colourful, and eccentric; McNally's is beautiful despite – or perhaps *because of* —- all the hardships the business endured.

There is just *something about* booksellers…

Books bought: 2

Copies of *Stroll* found: 0

Coffees consumed: 1

The Ones That Got Away

Throughout my many brief trips to Toronto, I managed to visit 27 bookstores. A bookseller at one of them expressed surprise that there *were* 27 – but there are actually more than that. Back in 1996, Arthur Wenk published a book called *A Guide to the Bookstores of Toronto.* It is now out of print, (and I never saw it in any of the used bookstores I visited), but the book apparently lists 250 stores in the Greater Toronto Area. I was not covering the entire GTA, so I hope that my mere 27 adequately represents the portions of the city centre that I did get around. Certainly, I didn't succeed in my quest to find *all* of them. Budget and timing did not align in some cases and so I have no doubt missed some amazing stores along the way. To these places, I sincerely apologise. Some of them, I don't even know about. Some of them I am aware of and couldn't get to. Unfortunately, most of the latter seem to be in the east end.

I loved the Danforth area and I thoroughly enjoyed being at the beach, too. Living in Saskatchewan means being landlocked. We are at the furthest point from either ocean in Canada and my daughter has never seen the sea. Lake Ontario is the next best thing; there are boats and sand and gulls stealing your lunch, and somehow it even smells salty and sealike, even though the lake is freshwater. I met a large raccoon behind the recycling bin at the ferry terminal when heading to Toronto Island, and it was one of the highlights of my trip. Having been severely distracted by those experiences, I lapsed and missed a few beachside and eastern bookstores.

The first bookstore I know I missed is a used bookstore in the east end on Kingston Road called The Great Escape. It has been in business for fifty years, and so is a contemporary of Glad Day Books in the downtown core. It is also the only bookstore I know of that has a rose garden in the back.

One that I really regret missing was Ella Minnow Books, also located on Kingston Road in the Fallingbrook area. I wanted to get there specifically because I realised that at no point on my voyage had I visited a children's bookstore. Some of the stores had excellent children's sections but I had not encountered an exclusively 'kid lit' store yet.

I did encounter Ella Minnow Books at the Toronto Word on the Street festival (called 'WOTS'). The bookseller had bright pink hair and did a great job of convincing me to visit properly. I promised I would, someday, but regretfully my visit will not be in time to appear in this book. I am not entirely sure who the eponymous Ella Minnow is, but I assume she's the owner. The store's website promises a Diversity and Inclusion booklist and a Gender Diversity and Equity booklist, and it has a whole section of its webstore dedicated to "Little Goodies." I look forward to finding it one day.

At this point I should mention Mabel's Fables. Mabel's is a long way north near Eglinton and Mount Pleasant. According to Google maps it is a 31-minute bike ride or a 42-minute metro ride in each direction. Unfortunately, I have never had the time nor opportunity to make that journey. I am curious as to whether Mabel's Fables is named after *Mabel Murple*. *Mabel Murple* is a children's book by Maritimes author Sheree Fitch. It was one of the first books I ever borrowed from Regina Public Library when we moved here and all my books were still in a shipping container crossing the Atlantic. Milo, then just two years old, absolutely loved the book. Mabel Murple lives in an entirely purple world. Given my tastes in both clothing and interior decor, I imagine Milo could easily relate to the book. I read it so often as a bedtime story that I think I can still recite parts of it from memory. Author Sheree Fitch owns a purple painted bookstore in Nova Scotia, called Mabel Murple's Book Shoppe & Dreamery, but to my knowledge she has not expanded into Toronto. This either means that Mabel's Fables is *inspired* by Mabel Murple, or, more likely, is owned by someone named Mabel. I fervently hope it is the former.

Moving outside of children's books, the other things sadly missing in my Bookstore Odyssey were Indigenous bookstores, and in fact, many BIPOC-owned stores. I was disappointed to find that although many of the places I visited had large ranges of Indigenous-authored books, none of them were Indigenous-owned. I did see a few Asian-owned bookstores, particularly around Kensington Market and Chinatown, including Sun Wa Bookstore that deals in used books in simplified Chinese. There is also Good Egg, which sells cookbooks only. A Different

Booklist on Bloor Street West is proudly Black-owned and I'm glad I got to that one. There is also Nile Valley Books, on Gerrard Street East, annoyingly close to where I explored, but sadly a bit further east than I managed. Nile Valley is another Black-owned store and is apparently "filled with African history." Like Ella Minnow, it has a sizable children's section. A few blocks from that is a place called Islamic Books and Souvenirs where you can buy children's books in Arabic. I regret missing all of these.

Outside of the East end, I also skipped several comic bookstores. This was a deliberate decision on my part; I have nothing against comic books, but I feel for the sake of this narrative, they would be out of place. I would not find copies of *Stroll* in them. I did pass many of these stores that all looked a little similar to my untrained eye: black painted signs with white text, boxes of comics outside for 50 cents each, and a lot of vinyl records as well as comics. They also seemed to have names that were memorable, if only because the names told you nothing about the contents of the store. Closest to my hostel was The Beguiling, which still insisted customers wore masks to enter the store; quite a rarity in 2024. I also encountered more than one branch of She Said Boom! The exclamation point was definitely not optional. Finally, in the north end was a store called ZOINKS! Zoinks is an excellent word, and of the three, the name that lent itself best to a comic store.

I am certain there are others. I did spot at least one ex-bookstore. It was an empty unit with a sign still up for a now-defunct business. This was on Yonge Street and I noticed it while walking back from Glad Day Books. Yonge Street is exceptionally long, so I imagine there are probably many others either closed or just hidden from me somewhere along that street. Not wishing to venture too far up Yonge for fear of never getting back down again in the traffic, I concentrated on Toronto's downtown core. This came at the expense of visiting Scarborough, Etobicoke, and Eglington – inspiration enough for a sequel to this book. Suburban bookstores may be a different world entirely. Like most big cities, Toronto eats other towns as it grows. Shawn Micallef had to update his *Stroll* book after fourteen years, and it took him eight months to re-walk the city as so much has changed. The overwhelming impression I got from my travels was that the outlook for independent bookstores is generally positive, but that Toronto is in a constant flux – and yes, I am aware that is an oxymoron, but it fits too well. Who knows, if I wait a few years, there may be a whole collection of new stores awaiting discovery.

Part 5: Toronto and Beyond

This Flâneuse has achy feet

A note in my journal from early January reads: *'Can I survive with one pair of shoes?'*

I am adept now at packing frugally. I knew this winter trip to Toronto was going to be short. The original purpose of the trip was to attend the trade show anyway, and so I wore my one pair of vaguely respectable heeled boots and thought that would be enough. At the time, I had little intention of walking half a marathon around Toronto's bookstores as well. The heels were not a good idea.

The point of the psychogeographic *dérive,* the semi-conscious drift through a city, is that it is unplanned. It should not have to require special shoes or advanced packing. My walk was not entirely aimless as I followed my list of bookstores, but it was at least spontaneous. My feet suffered as a result. I'm sure the original *flâneurs* of Paris (an 'idler,' saunterer, or wanderer) –
or even their modern-day equivalent like Shawn Micallef – did not worry about footwear.

This may be because they are mainly men. (Not to suggest that women can't wear comfortable shoes – I am usually in my beloved Doc Martens – but it is not always the default.) So far, I've come across very few psychogeography books written by women. A female *flâneur* is a *flâneuse,* and they do exist; Laura Elkin writes about walking in London, Paris, Venice, and New York. In a Canadian context, Tanis MacDonald wrote her 'adventures in walking while female' in her book, *Straggle.* But they are few and far between.

Walking alone as a woman in any city – particularly one that is not familiar – can be a complex and often challenging experience. I can walk the same streets as Shawn Micallef, I can follow all the routes he mentions in *Stroll*, but I will never see the environment in the same way he does. This is true of anyone of any gender or race of course; lived experience is by definition personal and subjective.

The ability to wander comes with prerequisites, however. You must be physically capable; I would have been able to cover much greater distances if I was fitter and healthier and even if I'd just slept better and worn sensible shoes. I have yet to find any psychogeographic writings from a wheelchair user, but I'm sure the results of that would be fascinating, eye-opening, and quite sobering. Traversing the city at pedestrian speed forces you to slow down and think about what you are seeing and feeling. I found it also made me take notice of how many things I take for granted. The existence of wide sidewalks, for instance, and my ability to climb stairs or keep my balance on ice.

A flâneur must also have the financial means: a smart phone for general safety and emergency calls, and in my case, as a way of accessing maps of bookstores and GPS to keep track of where I was and where I was heading. Walking is the cheapest form of transport and cycling is the most efficient, but a level of disposable income is also crucial. I could afford Presto cards that allowed me to jump on and off public transit when I needed to. I could buy myself coffee and snacks to fuel my excursions. I knew that if I ever really got completely stuck, I could afford to call a taxi to take me back to my room at the hostel.

Finally, a wanderer must have a sense of personal safety, the reassurance that you have the right to exist alone in public spaces. This is the requirement that rapidly becomes gendered and racialized. In Toronto, the right to be out in public is a given. No one was going to stop me from walking around, but that is not the same thing as feeling safe and comfortable while doing so. There are certainly areas of the city that would not be as safe to wander in as others, but as a naive outsider, I have no idea where these areas actually are and so I didn't know to fear them. I also would not undertake these wanderings at night. Although it goes against the traditions of psychogeography, I was always careful never to get truly lost.

Cities are not built for women because most were not built by women. I often equate the female experience of existing in public spaces to cycling on main roads. Like cyclists, we have every right to be there, but like cyclists we must be constantly vigilant and acutely aware of our surroundings at all times. Most people are not actively hostile towards us, but there are always an aggressive few who feel we should not exist in that space and do not want to share the roads with us.

We are either too visible – attracting unwanted attention and feeling too 'on display' in public areas – or we are invisible: not taken into account in urban planning and design. This becomes apparent in everything from the tendency of city planners to add dark, narrow underpasses for pedestrians, which often make it more dangerous to cross the street than running across three lanes of traffic would be. Or the lack of public bathrooms in city centres. I visited many Tim Hortons branches on my travels, not because I like their coffee, but just because I needed the toilet and Timmies was the only option.

My first experiences of Toronto were marred by trying to navigate around the city with my young children. Whilst this issue is not exclusive to women – and shouldn't be – it is worth noting that Toronto seems a very different place if your travelling companion is only three feet tall, can't walk more than a few blocks without complaining, and needs a nap every afternoon.

Instagram informs me that Shawn Micallef is now a proud new dad. I'm interested in seeing how his walks change now that he is pushing a stroller along with him. I fully expect there to be more ranting about the state of the sidewalks.

Despite the common narrative of women feeling unsafe in urban environments, my experiences walking around Toronto were peaceful and uneventful. Only a few incidents stood out. The first was during the Toronto Festival of Authors when I attempted to cycle from Harbourfront to the Junction neighbourhood to get to the Famous Last Words bar. I was lost at night, I was tired, and I was entirely alone a long way from anywhere I recognised. But at no point was I ever fearful – merely frustrated that I'd got myself into that situation in the first place.

The final night of TIFA was the Toronto Poetry Slam at the Harbourfront Theatre. I had met a friendly fellow festival attendee during the day, Stephanie. She was not a Toronto resident any longer, but she did know the city much better than I did, and I was glad of her company for the day. She had opted to see a different event in the evening, so I was on my own for the poetry slam. I watched fifteen poets perform that night, all highly talented individuals with different styles and from a wide range of backgrounds. Their poetry was powerful and compelling. Of the performances, eight of the women (and one man) had written about sexual assault. I have been to many emotionally charged poetry slams over the years and I was prepared for a degree of creative angst, but not on that scale. I left feeling shaken, anxious, and a little tearful. For the first time, I was wary about getting back to the hostel, alone in the dark.

It was a Friday night and the first time all week that it hadn't rained. The streets were busy. A group of loud, rowdy teenagers on the corner made me quicken my pace. As I neared the transit stop on Queens Quay, someone tapped me on the shoulder and made me jump nervously. It was Stephanie! She asked where I was going, and then helpfully explained that if I crossed over to York Street, I could get a bus that would take me right to the east end of Danforth Avenue where the hostel was, as opposed to catching a streetcar and then two different metro trains. She even accompanied me for most of the journey. I don't think she ever realised how grateful I was for her presence that night.

Back at the hostel, I decided to have a drink at the bar to unwind a little. And of course, that was the night someone tried to chat me up! Life is nothing if not ironic. The whole exchange caught me completely unawares. At forty, I was one of the oldest hostel dwellers there. I thought I was well past the point of attracting attention from anyone, least of all a good looking and very street-smart twenty-something. Fortunately, he was the perfect gentleman, accepted my polite 'No' for an answer and was generally charming enough that I was more flattered than intimidated by the encounter.

These experiences lead me to believe that Toronto is a relatively safe city – at least, for someone like me. I am privileged in that I have the ability, the means, and the aptitude to wander around cities by myself despite lacking any sense of direction and whilst making questionable decisions about cycling at night. The contrast with my small hometown is stark: the sheer number of people in Toronto is overwhelming after a decade in the vast and empty prairie. There is a reassuring safety in numbers, however, and I felt less vulnerable walking along the crowded streets near the CN Tower than I do stomping through the eerie quietness of Regina's downtown core.

Overall, I absolutely loved Toronto. By far the worst and most humbling part of my wanderings was just the agony caused by my idiotic choice of footwear.

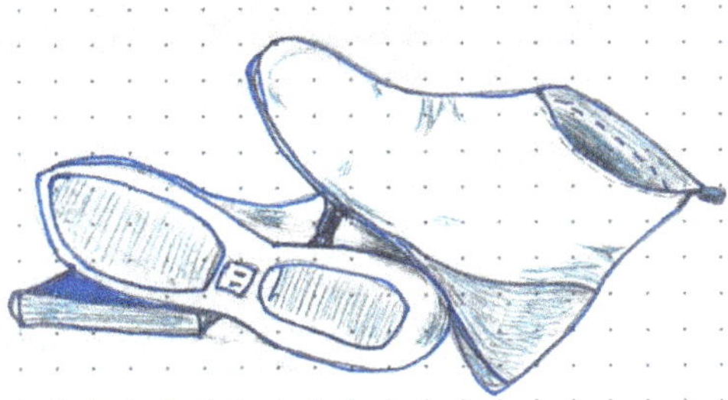

Cheating at Spacing

Of course, I did eventually find *Stroll*. But I do feel like I cheated in doing so.

I did not find the original 2010 version of *Stroll* in any of the two dozen or more bookstores I visited. I could have searched harder in some of the more crammed used bookstores, but I'm fairly certain the book was not in any of them. I did not see it anywhere until the new edition was released in the spring of 2024. Plenty of places offered to order it in for me, but that would not have scratched the same itch. I needed to see it on the shelves somewhere in the wild.

Instead, I chose to follow Shawn Micallef, again. This would of course have been the much simpler option to begin with, but then, I would never have as many adventures as I do if I always took the easy option. As well as being a walker, writer, psychogeographer, and university tutor, Micallef is also one of the original editors of *Spacing* magazine. *Spacing* is a magazine founded in 2003 and designed to bring together discussions on urbanity in many forms – transit, public art, city planning, sustainability, and everything in between. The magazine ends up being largely about Toronto but there is now a Vancouver branch as well. Between the print magazine, the online blog, and now a podcast, it manages to situate Torontonian issues in a wider urban studies context.

One day, in the spirit of psychogeography and due to getting frustrated waiting for my bus to weave its way through downtown traffic, I alighted several stops away from the area I recognised and decided to try and make some sense of 'the touristy bit.' There are few bookstores in the financial and entertainment districts of Toronto (aside from a two-storey branch of Indigo-Chapters in the Eaton centre), and so I'd had little reason to walk around there previously. The CN Tower dominates everything, but as I usually rely on it to orientate myself, I found being right underneath it oddly confusing. I couldn't use my internal compass when I was standing beneath the magnet.

The adjoining Roger's Centre arena – the Blue Jays baseball stadium –was the reason my bus had gotten stuck. Throngs of blue-clad fans choked the streets in the surrounding area. Then I spied Union Station, equally packed with people coming and going or just getting immobilized by the crowds. In my experience, Union Station is an excellent place to avoid. It is possibly even more complicated to navigate around than London's huge King's Cross Station, but mercifully there are no Harry Potter fans hopelessly running into platform walls. I am not sure what the Canadian equivalent of that would be! The space age high rises that surround Union Station shone and glowed as the afternoon drew on, and it truly felt like I was in a sci-fi fantasy novel. If Harry Potter has the monopoly on King's Cross, we are in dire need of a heroic teenager to find a magical way of escaping Union Station. He would have to have a raccoon as a Familiar.

Just a few blocks away, I did find myself in a completely different world. Here, the buildings were much lower and square, and red bricked rather than steel and glass and shiny. As I walked west, a man was having an animated argument with a tiny tree. (He appeared to have locked his bike to it with a heavy chain, and the chain had got caught in some tiny branches that had somehow offended him.) Someone else struggled to cross the road with an unwieldy stroller; the pedestrian crossing lights were extraordinarily badly timed, and there was no dropped curb to allow the stroller back onto the sidewalk. From the opposite side, two women stood with a rack of Bible study leaflets, ignoring the shrieking toddler in the stroller, and in turn, being ignored by the other passers-by. This area felt far more 'human.' As soon as I got out from under the high rises and the street returned to being human-scaled, I was suddenly able to start noticing things again. Specifically, I noticed that I could smell the wonderful scent of fresh coffee.

And then, I noticed a small, black, circular sign hanging out over the sidewalk. It said 'Spacing.' I was intrigued.

In 2014, *Spacing* magazine spawned a store of its own. Located right in the centre of the city on Richmond Street and sharing a building with an art gallery and studios, the coffee bar that I'd smelled, and a 'design' store, Spacing sells all things Toronto. There were cuddly raccoon toys, art prints of Toronto street scenes, public library tote bags, models of the streetcars, and stickers of anything even remotely related to the city. It is essentially a souvenir store or a place to show off your civic pride, but there are books! This was enough for me to justify a visit.

Most of these books were of the 'coffee table' variety – beautiful photo books of historical sites or architectural guides. I did get minorly side-tracked finding a book about Casa Loma, the castle north of Spadina Avenue. I would dearly like to know why there is a giant fairy tale castle inexplicably overlooking Toronto but sadly that one was beyond my budget at the time. I also found fiction books set in the city – *Scarborough* by Catherine Hernandez and my beloved *Denison Avenue* by Christina Wong amongst many others. *Spacing* writers and founders have also authored many books themselves; Shawn Micallef was no exception.

Even in the official Spacing store though, *Stroll* was not out on display. The updated version had not yet been released, so it was no surprise that the store was not showing off a twelve-year-old book. But finally, here was somewhere where the booksellers actually knew what I was talking about. I explained my mission to the man behind the counter as best I could, mentioning my fruitless search, my aching feet, and the fact that despite my accent, I had come from Saskatchewan. He looked bewildered. It was a familiar expression now.

"Do you know Shawn?" he asked.

I shook my head and it began to dawn on me precisely how unhinged I must have sounded. I assured him that my fanaticism was entirely literary based. Still giving me wary looks, the man called for a colleague, and then disappeared out of sight of the main store. Momentarily I panicked that he was calling security. I waited, awkwardly, for what seemed like hours, but then he reappeared, smiling. He was holding a copy of *Stroll*.

"We don't have many left," he apologised. "Did you hear there's a new version coming out soon? You might want to wait for that." Again, I shook my head. This was the one I wanted! I was overjoyed, irrationally excited. I practically threw the last of my cash at him and ran out, determined to get back to my hostel bunk to fully admire my new treasure as quickly as possible.

That night, my celebrations were muted by exhaustion; my phone informed me that my little psychogeographic *dérive* towards Spacing that day had actually been close to eleven kilometres by the time I got back to the hostel. I kicked my shoes off gleefully, had a solitary beer in the bar, and began to read.

It was a shame that I never found this book in a traditional bookstore, and going to Spacing did feel a little like cheating. I never managed to see the book – or Shawn Micallef – 'in the wild.' But then, this mission was entirely self-defined. If my goals were to find indie bookstores, buy a copy of the original *Stroll,* and take in and explore as much of Toronto as I could in a very limited amount of time, then I had certainly achieved them.

When I write, I am a 'pantser' – that is, I rarely plan out anything in advance, and write 'by the seat of my pants.' I start somewhere, vague and hopeful, and see where the story takes me. This particular story had taken me 2,600 kilometres from home, four times, and introduced me to so many vibrant new characters; the British barista at Fahrenheit Coffee, jazz bands and tattoos and icecream with hostel companions, Stephanie the writer, the hot twenty-something who flattered my ego in a bar, and so many booksellers and booklovers in all the stores I found along the way. And then there were some famous cameos from the Festival of Authors as well. When I consider the journey as a whole, the Spacing store did feel like a satisfying conclusion to the adventure.

Like everything else that I enjoy, it was not what I expected, but it was exactly what I needed.

The Shelf Life of Optimism

It would have been The Penny University Bookstore's fourth birthday in September 2024. I say 'would have' because the bookstore is now gone.

I just couldn't do it anymore.

For four years, my bookstore had been my whole world. I live just two blocks away from it, so the space became almost an extension of my own house. I used to joke that my To Be Read pile grew so large at home that I had no choice but to open up shop. My children would end up there after school every time I worked late – or more frequently, whenever Milo forgot his door key. Our cat took up residence in the store as our 'Head of Marketing.' My store manager filmed videos for her Youtube channel there, after hours. The local daycare did 'field trips' to the store, marching a dozen three-year-olds in for Storytime long after my own children aged out and started school. My friends gathered there for our book group in the evenings. People came in, not always to browse books, but often just to chat to me or my staff as we provided a friendly space in between appointments, or on the school-run, or in which to shelter from Saskatchewan's extremes of temperature.

It took time, but my store gradually became a refuge where readers could lose themselves in stories and catch a break from the chaos of life during and post-pandemic. Like many of the bookstores I visited in Toronto, we quickly became a hub, not just for book lovers and writers, but for the local queer community, and, perhaps inevitably, for the small Progressive contingent in Regina. Our most well-attended event was a book launch for *A Healthy Future*, written by the former leader of the provincial

NDP, Dr. Ryan Meili. This was closely followed by the launch of a book about labour unions and the local Co-Op Refinery. Our biggest fiction event was for a non-binary author whose Young Adult novel is loosely based on the tales of King Arthur, but with queer and trans characters and set in downtown Vancouver. I have always appreciated the sheer variety of books that came our way through the bookstore, especially in a city as small as Regina.

Yet, as with many independent bookstores across Canada, the dream that once fuelled my endeavour has reached its sombre end. Our events were wonderful, the people who came to visit us to chat were lovely, so were the daycare outings, and the book groups… but none of those things ever made us much money. A particularly blunt friend of mine once pointed out that unless I was actually making a profit, I didn't have a business, I had an expensive hobby. That remark stung me enough to stay with me long after I lost touch with her. In the summer of 2024, I had to face the fact that the bookstore was not only an expensive hobby, it was rapidly turning into a financial black hole. The time had come to cut my losses and say goodbye.

Even with a mountain of debt hanging over me, the decision to close was not made lightly. Every book that adorned our shelves, every event we hosted, every customer who walked through the door was a testament to my team's commitment and love for the literary world. We had hoped to offer a space that transcended mere retail; I had named the bookstore after places where ideas could be exchanged. The original Penny Universities were the coffee houses of 17th century London. Places, it was said, where you could get a university education for the price of a one-penny cup of coffee just by listening to the animated conversations and debates that took place within them. I'd wanted to build a place where local authors could thrive and where readers could find a sense of belonging. In those respects, I had succeeded. Yet, despite my best efforts, I found myself grappling with financial realities that no amount of passion could overcome.

For most, as I found continuously in Toronto, the dream of running an independent bookstore is a labour of love. That love can be for the books themselves, as evidenced by the array of used, rare, and antiquarian book collectors and dealers I met. Or it can be a personal mission, such as the founders of A Different Booklist trying to preserve and showcase the history of their community, or the owners of Caversham Books educating people on mental health issues. Different again were the 'themed' bookstores, the horror books at Little Ghosts, the sci-fi wonderland at Re:Reading, and even the love of all things oceanic at Nautical Minds. All the bookstores in Toronto were very different, but the owners were united by their passion for literature.

I can't imagine many of them getting into this business solely for the money, because we all know there's very little of that. In Toronto, I wasn't hunting specifically for methods of making a quick buck for my store; I had started my bookstore odyssey looking for *hope.* I wanted to find inspiration from my fellow store owners and comradery around the challenges we all face. I found it in abundance.

But then, I thought again of Ben McNally's store having to move out from its original, beautiful location. BMV cutting its cafe hours down to the bare minimum. Glad Day Books having to crowdfund to stay afloat. These literary labours of love are often accompanied by personal sacrifice and we were no exception to this. I did not take a salary in four years and felt guilty if I dared take a day off. I poured everything I had – my time, energy, and money into creating a space that would enrich our community, only to find that it wasn't enough. It would never be enough. The financial strain was relentless and bibliophilia alone does not pay the bills.

The independent bookstore industry in Canada has long been a challenging one. Small bookstores face myriad obstacles: competition from online giants, fluctuating economic conditions, the ever-rising costs of operation, oh, and global pandemics. For me, it was the Canada Emergency Business Account (CEBA) loan that was the killing blow. I had felt so relieved when I was able to pay it off in January by refinancing, but in doing so, all I had achieved was a delay to the inevitable. Debt is the ultimate passion-killer, creeping up on you until it gets the chance to bleed you dry. It is a slow and painful death.

Running out of money was not just a practical issue, it was deeply personal. Each tax return, each credit card statement felt like a harsh reminder of the fragility of my dream. I watched as our revenue fell short of our expenses, despite our best efforts to adapt and innovate. Events that once drew crowds now struggled to attract attendees, and the influx of new book releases, while exciting, failed to translate into the financial stability we desperately needed.

The closing of The Penny University Bookstore is not unique; it is emblematic of a broader trend within the industry. There is an argument to be made that the vanishing of spaces like mine reflects a broader shift in how we interact with literature and culture in an increasingly digital and commercialised world. But I am not going to make that argument myself. My experience with my bookstore, and my trip around the similar stores in Toronto has taught me the opposite – it is *not* the case that people don't read any more. *Some* people appear to be reading more than ever. I did have a great many loyal, returning customers. But I had far more of them when I put the books on sale.

Books are one of life's little luxuries – a chance to slow down and learn something, find a new way to fall in love, or enjoy a dash of escapism. I often benefited from impulse purchases – it is difficult for many to enter a bookstore and leave with *just one* book. Even those organised people who pre-ordered new releases and came in, beaming and proud, to collect their orders on Publication Day, would leave with many other books that happened to catch their eye on the way to my cash desk. However, as these tough economic times become more pronounced, when people are struggling to buy groceries or put gas in their car, spending $35 on a new hardcover book becomes far less of a priority. Books are necessary for an enjoyable life, but not as necessary as paying your rent.

As I prepared to shut our doors, my staff and I were filled with a profound sense of loss. It is a loss for the community that embraced us, for the authors whose works we championed, and for ourselves, who dreamed of making a difference through the simple act of sharing books. I have spent considerable time recently wandering around Regina, slowly processing my grief. The small city means I walk the same neighbourhoods that my bookstore served. The freeing anonymity I feel in the crowded streets of Toronto cannot exist here: too many people know me. I see the concern on their faces, the looks of pity. As I head to my favourite coffee shop, the local plumber sees me and crosses the street to give me a hug. The barista gives me a hefty discount on my Americano. One of the authors whose books I stocked is sitting in the coffee shop with her laptop, hard at work editing her next novel. She gifts me an advanced reader copy of it.

"You probably don't need any more books right now." She grins apologetically. "I just wanted you to have this. Thank you for all you've done for us starving artists."

Even in this moment of sorrow, choked as I am, I recognise the value of the experience we gained. The friendships forged, the stories shared, and the impact we had, however fleeting, are all part of a legacy that extends beyond the closing of the bookstore.

As I close this chapter, I do so with gratitude for the support we received and with hope for the future. While my bookstore may be gone, the stories and experiences I shared with the bookstore owners I met during my journey across Toronto will continue to resonate. The independent bookstore industry may be fraught with challenges and not all of us can survive. Those that do – and they are numerous – form a testament to the enduring power of literature and community. In the quiet after the final sale at The Penny University Bookstore, I find solace in the knowledge that there are spaces where books, and the people who love them, continue to matter.

Books bought (for The Penny University Bookstore, 2020-2024): ~25,000

Local Authors who stocked their books with us: 92

Book Launches hosted: 53

Copies of *Stroll* now owned: 2

Coffees consumed: *(incalculable, but an unhealthy amount nonetheless)*

Part 6: End Notes

Psycho-Cartography?

As previously mentioned, I spent a great deal of time in Toronto not quite sure where I was. On the odd occasion where I had a definite destination in mind, I relied heavily on Google Maps on my phone rather than traditional paper maps of the city. Walking along following Google's blue arrow gives you no concept of the distances involved, as the scale of the map changes depending on how far you zoom in. Similarly, the advised travel times do not take into account the minor detours when I saw something interesting, breaks to get coffee, or the time it took to get the bike share app working each time.

I tried to reflect the subjectivity of distance and direction in my own maps and divided the city into four wonky and arbitrarily-sized compass quadrants. There is no consistent scale on these, but if somewhere felt like a really long walk to get to, I drew it a long way from my starting point. As a rough guide, the Harbourfront to Queen's Park near the University of Toronto is about twenty minutes due north on a bike. The hostel in Kensington Market to Gerrard Street East (a few blocks north of Queen Books - #20) took 54 minutes on a streetcar. Spadina at College to Roncesvalle is about a half hour cycle ride. What I considered the longest and least enjoyable walk was Monkey's Paw Books (#17 on the North Map) to Type Books (#26 on the South map) below Trinity Bellwoods Park, which took me over an hour even when I gave up and caught a bus. Geographically, the furthest point west (Famous Last Words, #13) to the furthest east (#10, Circus Books) is just over 13 kilometres.

Over the course of my four trips, I walked over 60 kilometres bookstore-hunting, cycled at least half that again, and lost track of my bus rides. In short, the following maps are for illustration purposes only and should not be relied on if you are lost. But I do hope you enjoy them as much as I enjoyed drawing them.

MAP LEGEND:

1. A Different Booklist, 779 Bathurst St., Toronto, ON M5S 0B7

2. A Good Read, 341 Roncesvalles Ave., Toronto, ON M6R 2M8

3. Another Story Bookshop, 315 Roncesvalles Ave., Toronto, ON M6R 2M6

4. Bakka-Phoenix 84 Harbord St., Toronto, ON M5S 1G5

5. Balfour Books 468 College St., Toronto, ON M6G 1A1

6. Ben McNally's Books, 108 Queen St. E., Toronto, ON M5C 1S4

7. BMV 471 Bloor St. W., Toronto, ON M5S 1X9

8. Book City, 348 Danforth Ave., Toronto, ON M4K 1N8

9. Caversham Books, 98 Harbord St., Toronto, ON M5S 1G6

10. Circus Books, 866 Danforth Ave., Toronto, ON M4J 1L7

11. David Mason Books, 366 Adelaide St. W. Suite LL05, Toronto, ON M5V 1R9

12. Doug Miller Books, 650 Bloor St. W., Toronto, ON M6G 1K9

13. Famous Last Words, 392 Pacific Ave., Toronto, ON M6P 2R1

14. Flying Books, 784 College St., Toronto, ON M6G 1C6

15. Glad Day Books, 499 Church St., Toronto, ON M4Y 2C6

16. Little Ghosts, 930 Dundas St. W., Toronto, ON M6J 1W3

17. Monkey's Paw, 1067 Bloor St. W., Toronto, ON M6H 3B9

18. Nautical Mind, 249 Queens Quay W. #108, Toronto, ON M5J 2N5

19. Penguin Random House, 320 Front St. W. #1400, Toronto, ON M5V 3B6

20. Queen Books, 914 Queen St. E., Toronto, ON M4M 1J5

21. Re: Reading, 548 Danforth Ave. Toronto, Ontario M4K 1P8

22. Scribe Books, 375 Danforth Ave., Toronto, ON M4K 1P1

23. Seekers Books, 509 Bloor St. W., Toronto, ON M5S 1Y2

24. Sellers and Newel, 672 College St., Toronto, ON M6G 1B9

25. Spacing Store, 401 Richmond St. W., Toronto, ON M5V 3A8

26. Type Books, 883 Queen St. W., Toronto, ON M6J 1G5

27. University of Toronto Bookstore, 214 College St., Toronto, ON M5T 3A1

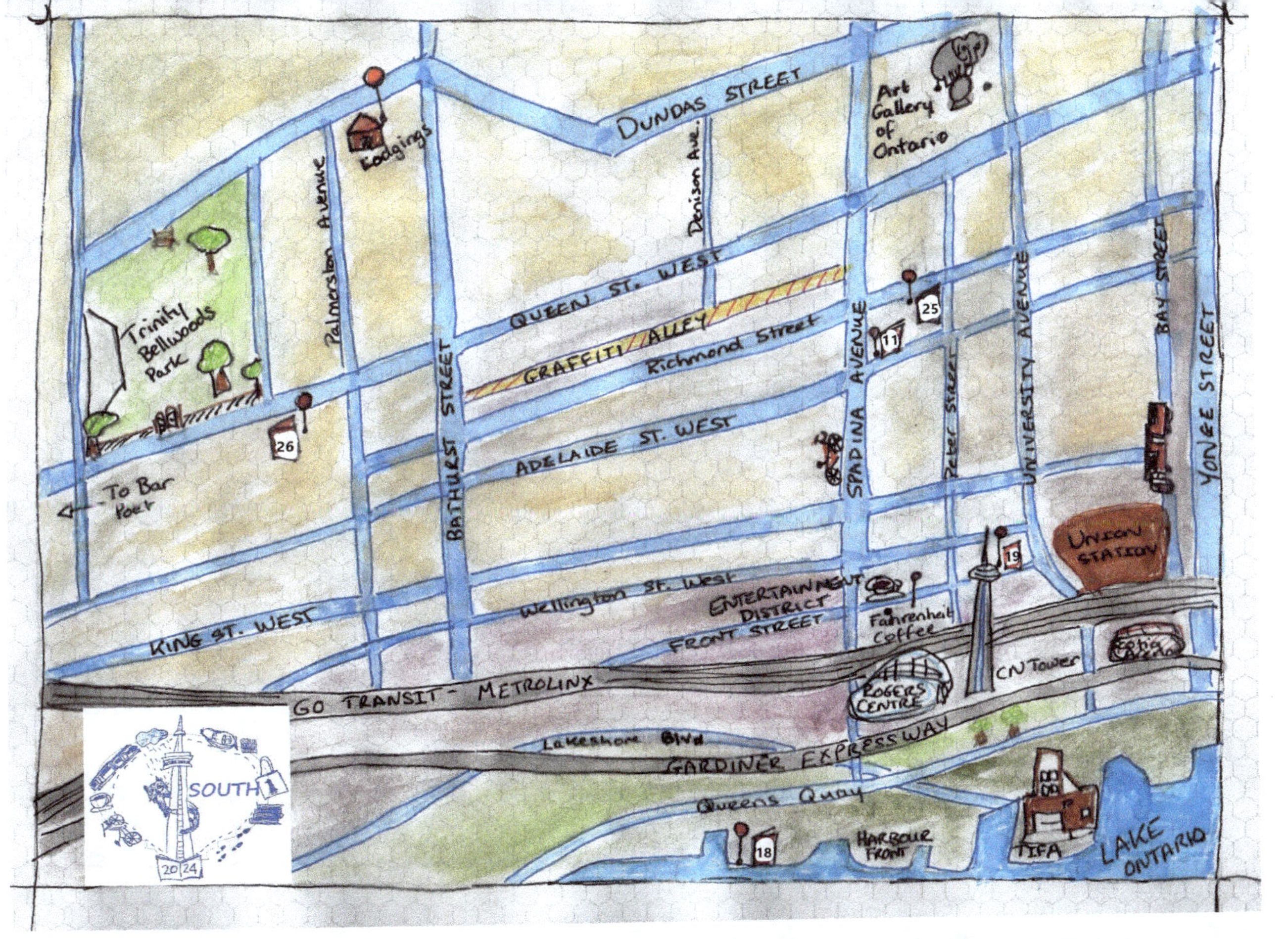
DUNDAS STREET
Art Gallery of Ontario
Lodgings
Palmerston Avenue
Denison Ave.
Trinity Bellwoods Park
QUEEN St. WEST
GRAFFITI ALLEY
Richmond Street
SPADINA AVENUE
25
11
Peter Street
University Avenue
BAY STREET
YONGE STREET
26
ADELAIDE St. WEST
To Bar Port
BATHURST STREET
Union Station
19
Wellington St. West
ENTERTAINMENT DISTRICT
FRONT STREET
Fahrenheit Coffee
CN Tower
KING St. WEST
GO TRANSIT - METROLINX
Rogers Centre
Lakeshore Blvd
GARDINER EXPRESSWAY
Queens Quay
18
HARBOUR FRONT
TIFA
LAKE ONTARIO
SOUTH
20 24

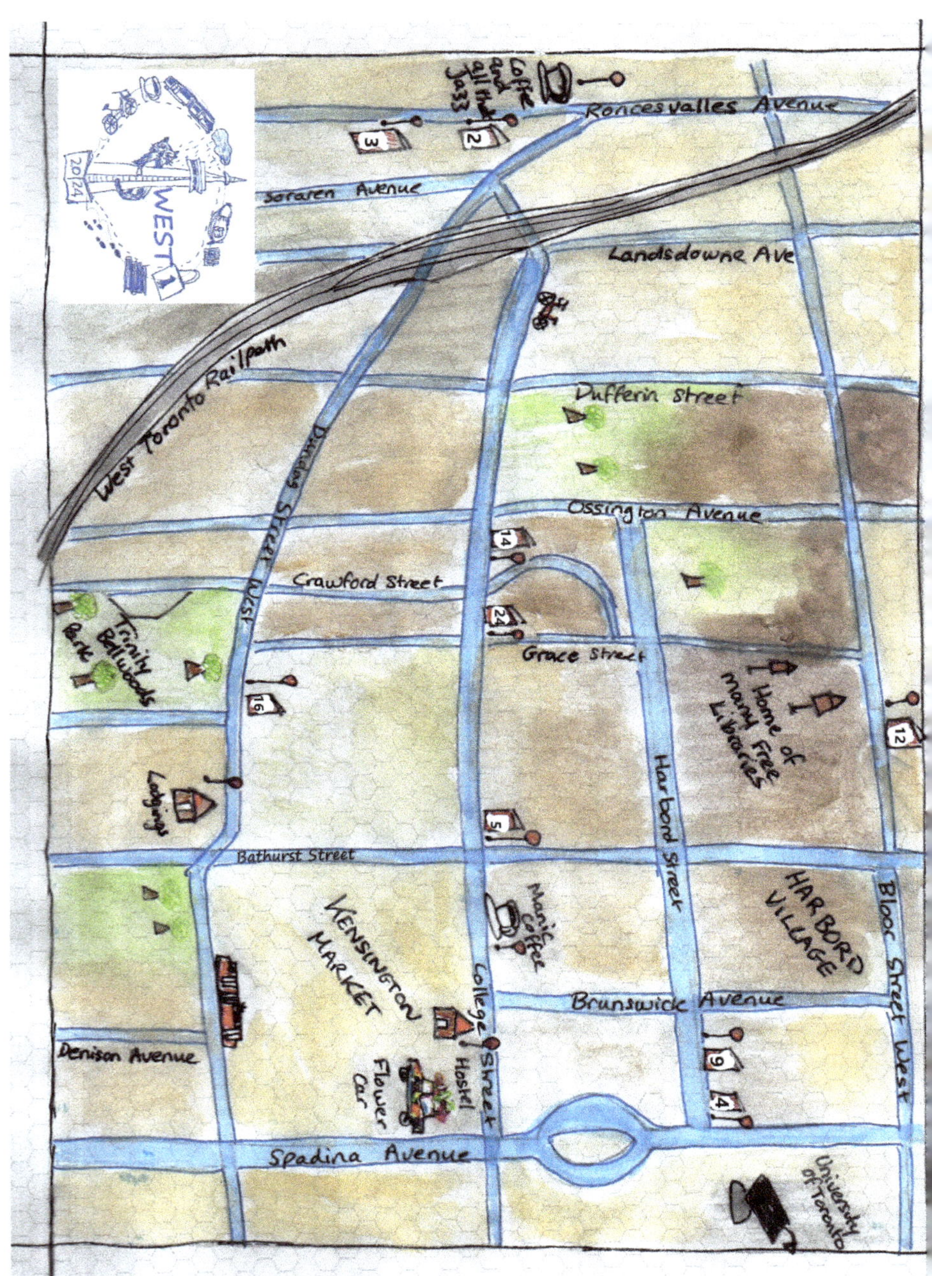
WEST
2024
1
Latte and all that Jazz
3
2
Roncesvalles Avenue
Soraren Avenue
Landsdowne Ave
West Toronto Railpath
Dufferin Street
Ossington Avenue
14
Crawford Street
24
Grace Street
Home of many Free Libraries
12
Trinity Bellwoods Park
16
Dundas Street West
Harbord Street
Lodgings
5
Bathurst Street
HARBORD VILLAGE
Bloor Street West
Kensington Market
Manic Coffee
Brunswick Avenue
9
Denison Avenue
College Street
Hostel
4
Flower Car
Spadina Avenue
University of Toronto

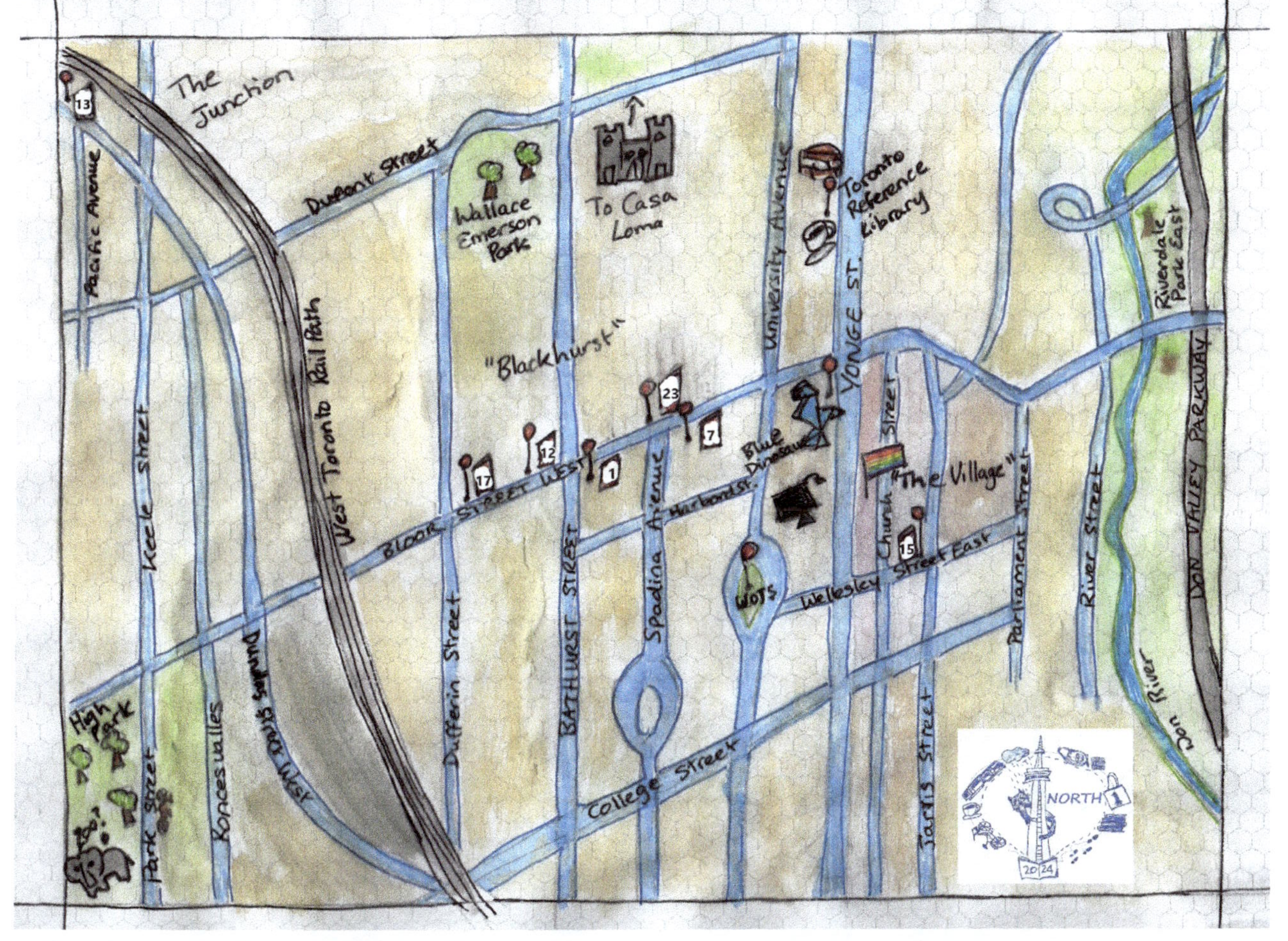
The Junction
13
Pacific Avenue
Dupont Street
Wallace Emerson Park
To Casa Loma
University Avenue
Toronto Reference Library
YONGE ST.
Riverdale Park East
"Blackhurst"
23
West Toronto Rail Path
7
12
Blue Dinosaur
Street
17
BLOOR STREET WEST
1
Spadina Avenue
Bathurst St.
Church Street
"The Village"
Parliament Street
River Street
DON VALLEY PARKWAY
Keele Street
BATHURST STREET
WOTS
15
Wellesley Street East
Don River
Dufferin Street
Dundas Street West
High Park
Park Street
Roncesvalles
College Street
Jarvis Street
NORTH
20 24

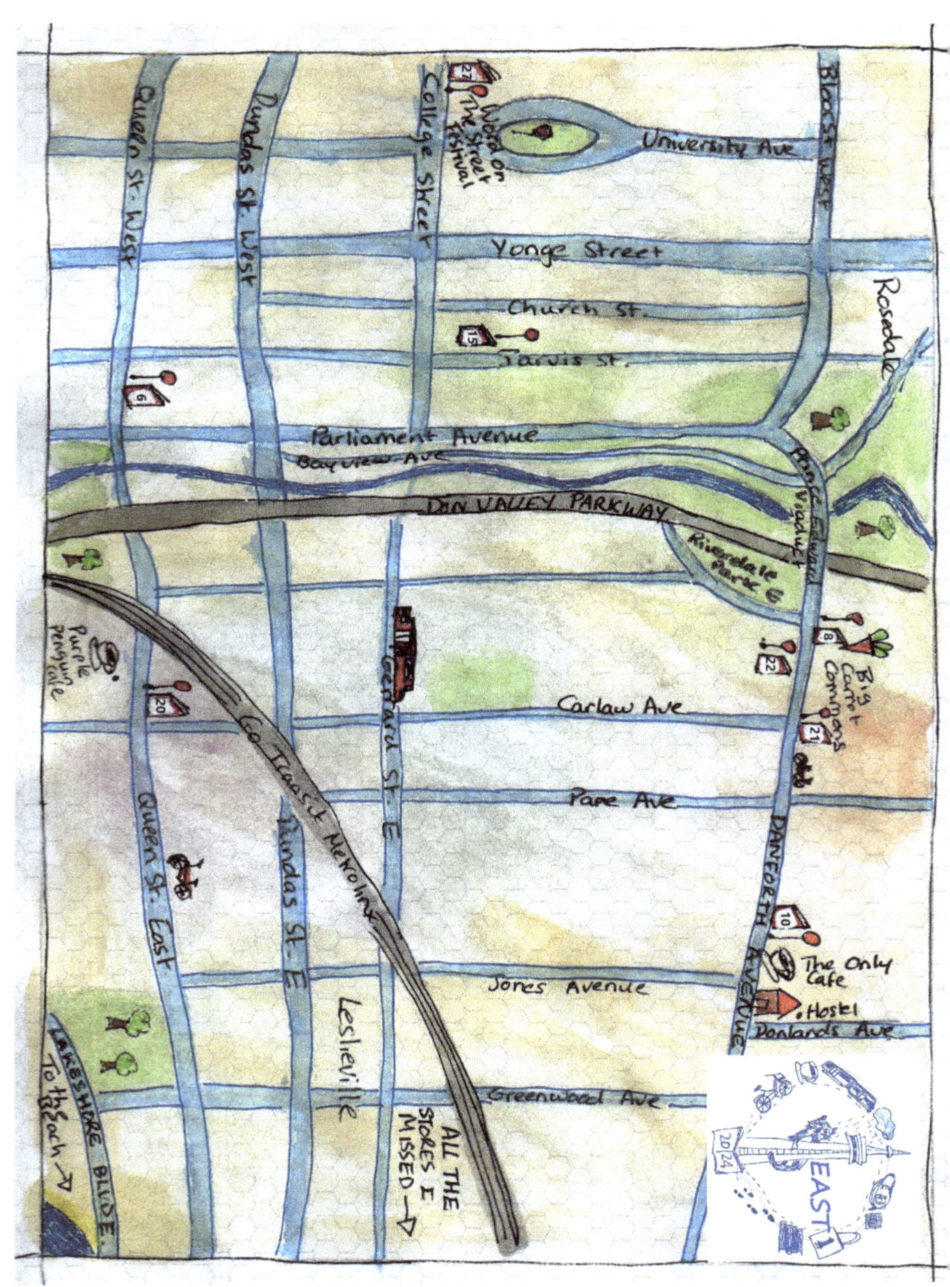
27
Word on
The Street
Festival
College Street
Dundas St. West
Queen St. West
Bloor St. West
University Ave
Rosedale
Yonge Street
Church St.
15
Jarvis St.
6
Parliament Avenue
Bayview Ave
Prince Edward Viaduct
DON VALLEY PARKWAY
Riverdale Park E
8
Big Carrot Commons
22
21
Carlaw Ave
Pape Ave
Purple Penguin cafe
20
Go Transit Metrolinx
Gerrard St. E
Queen St. East
Dundas St. E
Leslieville
Jones Avenue
DANFORTH AVENUE
10
The Only Cafe
Hostel
Donlands Ave
Greenwood Ave
ALL THE STORES I MISSED →
LAKESHORE BLVD E.
To the Beach →
20 24
EAST

Books Purchased On Route

50 Ways to Protect Bookstores by Danny Caine

A Lively Bit of the Front by Percy F. Westerman

Because of the Rabbit by Cynthia Lord

The Bicyclist's Guide to the Galaxy: Feminist, Fantastical Tales of Books and Bikes by Elly Blue

The Book of Delights by Ross Gay

Dragging Mason County by Curtis Campbell

Flash Forward: An Illustrated Guide to Possible and Not So Possible Tomorrows edited by Rose Eveleth

If I Were A Book by Jose Jorge Letria

Morantology by Caitlin Moran

Narwhal and Jelly Superpod Party Pack by Ben Clayton

The Penguin Book of the City edited by Robert Drewe

Psychotherapy - A Very Short Introduction by Tom Burns and Eva Burns Ludgren

Raising Steam by Terry Pratchett

Reuniting with Strangers by Jennilee Austria-Bonifacio

Skipper Tips for Every Day by Fridjof Gunkel

Wanderers, A History of Women Walking edited by Kerri Andrews

Welcome to Blackhurst, An Iconic Toronto Neighbourhood produced by A Different Publisher at the Blackhurst Cultural Centre.

Further Reading

Bibliomaniac by Robin Ince

Biketopia: Feminist Bicycle Science Fiction Stories in Extreme Futures edited by Elly Blue

The Dark Library by Cyrille Martinez (translated by Joseph Patric Stancil)

The Death and Life of Great American Cities by Jane Jacobs

Denison Avenue by Christina Wong and Daniel Innes

*Everything is F*cked, A Book About Hope* by Mark Mansun

Frontier City, Toronto on the Verge of Greatness by Shawn Micallef

A Guide to the Bookstores of Toronto by Arthur Wenk

How to Protect Bookstores and Why: the present and future of bookstores by Danny Caine

Psychogeography by Will Self and Ralph Steadman

A Splendor of Letters: The Permanence of Books in an Impermanent World by Nicholas A Basbanes

Subdivided: City Building in an Age of Hyper Diversity by John Lorinc

Walkable City by Jeff Speck

Wheeling Through Toronto, A history of the bicycle and its riders by Albert Koehl

Write the Neighbourhood edited by Shae Loeffelholz

Acknowledgements

Although my original motivation for this ridiculous quest was one of healing and a desire to escape Regina for a while, it soon snowballed into a multi-trip adventure the likes of which I could never have predicted. As such, I apologise for my carbon footprint that accumulated through multiple cross-country flights and paying excess baggage to bring all my books home. Had there been a less environmentally terrible means of travelling between Saskatchewan and Ontario, believe me I would have taken it.

None of these adventures would have been possible without my eternally patient and understanding husband, Carl. Not only is he entirely unfazed by me disappearing without him on these trips, he also runs around after the kids and our pets in my absence, mops me up when I wobble and fail, and still manages to work full time and bail me out of the occasional financial disaster. Without his unwavering support, I would never have the confidence to do half the things I do, be it in business or in life in general.

To Milo and Theia, who seem to have inherited my love of books. I am so very proud of everything you do.

To Mackenzie Brooks, Marin Waddell, and Hannah Rumble – my core crew who I can count on to cheer me on and support every obscure project I dream up. Please know that it is all so greatly appreciated.

Immense gratitude also goes to Robyn Dansereau: my editor, publishing partner, and most importantly, my equally-book-obsessed friend. It has been a steep learning curve, but an absolute pleasure beginning a new publishing venture with you. Thank you also for allowing me a few comma splices.

In Toronto, I was met with warm welcomes at the Dragon Gate Inn, The Only Backpackers Inn and in particular Planet Traveler, the staff at which heard most about this venture. Thank you to all who work there, and I am sorry for being rude about the coffee.

A great many authors inspired parts of this book: Shawn Micallef of course, and perhaps unbeknownst to them, Robin Ince for the bibliomania and Will Self for the laconic travel writing. Lapin, the French artist and illustrator, was my tutor for an online course in urban sketching. Thanks to him, my confidence in drawing was boosted enough to try my hand at illustrating this book. My perspective is wonky in spite of his careful instruction, not because of it.

Finally, I want to thank all the bookstore owners of Toronto that I met along the way. Thank you for sharing your experiences, your advice, and your time. You are all an incredible source of admiration and inspiration to me.

About the Author

Annabel Townsend is a life-long book lover, coffee aficionado, and stubborn cyclist. She has a PhD in geography and wrote her thesis about the coffee industry before opening her own coffee shop in the UK. She has now run small businesses on both sides of the Atlantic, most recently, The Penny University Bookstore in Regina, SK. A lot of these entrepreneurial adventures end up in her writing. She writes mainly nonfiction but occasionally dabbles with spoken word and sci-fi writing. She lives in Regina with her husband, kids, and a great many small animals.

Also by the Author:

Spilling the Beans: Concepts of Quality in the Speciality Coffee Industry (2012)

It Seemed Like A Good Idea At The Time: Ten Years of Misadventures in Coffee (2018)

A Thousand Lives: Pithy Essays from Bookshops, Coffee Pots and the Covid Crisis (2023)